STUDY GUIDE

The Watsons Go to Birmingham—1963

Christopher Paul Curtis

WITH CONNECTIONS

HOLT, RINEHART AND WINSTON
Harcourt Brace & Company

Austin • New York • Orlando • Atlanta • San Francisco • Boston • Dallas • Toronto • London

Staff Credits

Associate Director: Mescal Evler

Manager of Editorial Operations: Robert R. Hoyt

Managing Editor: Bill Wahlgren

Executive Editor: Emily Shenk

Book Editor: Mikki Gibson

Editorial Staff: *Assistant Managing Editor,* Mandy Beard; *Copyediting Supervisor,* Michael Neibergall; *Senior Copyeditor,* Mary Malone; *Copyeditors,* Joel Bourgeois, Jon Hall, Jeffrey T. Holt, Jane M. Kominek, Susan Sandoval; *Editorial Coordinators,* Marie H. Price, Jill Chertudi, Mark Holland, Marcus Johnson, Tracy DeMont; *Support Staff,* Pat Stover, Matthew Villalobos; *Word Processors,* Ruth Hooker, Margaret Sanchez, Kelly Keeley

Permissions: Carrie Jones, Catherine Paré

Design: *Art Director, Book & Media Design,* Joe Melomo

Image Services: *Art Buyer, Supervisor,* Elaine Tate

Prepress Production: Beth Prevelige, Sergio Durante

Manufacturing Coordinator: Michael Roche

Development Coordinator: Diane B. Engel

Cover Photo: (car) HRW Photo / Mavournea Hay; (map background) Courtesy of Michigan Department of Transportation; (people) HRW Photo / Sam Dudgeon; (young boy) Courtesy of the Alexander Family

HRW is a registered trademark licensed to Holt, Rinehart and Winston.

Printed in the United States of America

ISBN 0-03-054049-6

56 085 02 01 00

TABLE of CONTENTS

Using This Study Guide

This Study Guide is intended to

- *help students become active and engaged readers*
- *deepen students' enjoyment and understanding of literature*
- *provide you with multiple options for guiding students through the novel and the Connections and for evaluating students' progress*

Most of the pages in this Study Guide are reproducible so that you can, if you choose, give students the opportunity to work independently.

Key Elements

- plot summary and analysis
- major themes
- character summaries
- notes on setting, point of view, and other literary elements

Making Meanings

- First Thoughts
- Shaping Interpretations
- Connecting with the Text
- Extending the Text
- Challenging the Text

A **Reading Check** focuses on review and comprehension.

The Worksheets

- **Reading Skills and Strategies Worksheets** focus on reading and critical-thinking strategies and skills.
- **Literary Elements Worksheets** guide students in considering and analyzing literary elements (discussed in **Key Elements**) important to understanding the novel.
- **Vocabulary Worksheets** provide practice with Vocabulary Words. Activities target synonyms, affixes, roots, context clues, and other vocabulary elements.

For the Teacher

About the Writer Biographical highlights supplement the author biography that appears in the HRW Library edition of this novel. Sidebars list works by and about the writer as resources for teaching and for students' research.

About the Novel A critical history summarizes responses to the novel, including excerpts from reviews. Sidebars suggest audiovisual and multimedia resources.

Key Elements Significant literary elements of the novel are introduced. These elements recur in the questions, activities, worksheets, and assessment tools.

For the Student: reproducible masters

Before You Read: Activities *(preparation for beginning the novel)* Motivating activities lead students to explore ideas and topics they will encounter in the novel.

Making Meanings *(for each section of the novel)* Questions move students from immediate personal response to high-level critical thinking.

Choices: Building Your Portfolio *(for each section of the novel)* The activities suggested here involve students in exploring different aspects of the novel on their own or collaboratively. The results may be included in a portfolio, developed further, or used as springboards for larger projects.

Novel Projects *(culminating activities)* Cross-Curricular, Multimedia, and Internet projects relate to the novel as a whole. Project ideas can be adapted for individual, pair, or group presentations.

Exploring the Connections *(a set of Making Meanings questions for each of the Connections readings)* Questions encourage students to relate the readings to the themes and topics of the novel.

Novel Notes *(multiple issues)* These one-page news sheets provide high-interest background information relating to historical, cultural, literary, and other elements of the novel. They are intended for distribution *after* students have begun the novel section the issue supplements.

Reading Skills and Strategies Worksheets *(one for each section of the novel, plus a Novel Organizer)*

Literary Elements Worksheets *(end of novel)*

Vocabulary Worksheets *(during or after reading)*

Glossary, with Vocabulary Words *(to use throughout the novel)* This list of words from the novel serves as a mini-dictionary that students may refer to as they read. **Highlighted Vocabulary Words** support vocabulary acquisition.

Test *(end of novel)* A mix of objective and short-answer questions covering the whole novel provides a traditional form of assessment. Essay questions consist of five optional writing prompts.

Tips for Classroom Management

Preparing Students for Reading

Set aside a time each week for talking about books. On the right are some ideas for introducing a novel and motivating students to pick it up and begin reading.

Reading and Responding

Book groups Although most students will read independently, discussions with classmates can enrich their reading enormously. This Study Guide suggests appropriate points to stop and talk about the story so far. At these stopping points, the **Making Meanings** questions can be used as discussion starters. Ask groups to keep a simple log of their discussions.

Full-class discussions Engage students by beginning the discussion with a question that encourages a personal response (see **First Thoughts** in **Making Meanings**). As students respond to the questions involving interpretation, invite them to support their inferences and conclusions with evidence from the text. Encourage a noncritical environment. Show your own enthusiasm for the novel—it's infectious!

Reader's logs Logs, journals, and notebooks offer an open and nonthreatening yet systematic mode for students to respond in writing to the novel. Making entries as they read can help students learn more about themselves as readers, monitor their own progress, and write more easily and fluently. Keeping logs can also enhance participation in small-group and class discussions of the novel. Consider dialogue journals in which two readers—a student and you, a classmate, or a family member—exchange thoughts about their reading. **Reader's Log** suggestions appear in each issue of **Novel Notes.**

Cooperative learning Small groups may meet both to discuss the novel and to plan and work on projects related to the novel (see ideas in **Choices** and in **Novel Projects**). Encourage full participation by making sure that each group member has a defined role and that the roles rotate so that the same student is not always the leader or the recorder, for example.

Projects While students' projects can extend into other content areas, they should always contribute to enriching and extending students' understanding of the novel itself. If students know when they begin the novel that presenting a project will be a part of their evaluation, they can begin early to brainstorm, discuss, and try out ideas. Project ideas can come from **Novel Notes,** from the **Choices** activities, from the **Novel Projects** ideas, and, of course, from the students themselves. Projects can be developed and presented by individuals, pairs, or groups.

Reflecting

When students finish the novel, they should not be left with a test as the culminating experience. Project presentations can be a kind of celebration, as can a concluding discussion. On the right are some ideas for a reflective discussion. They can be used in a whole-class environment, or small groups can choose certain questions to answer and share their conclusions (or their disagreements) with the class.

Ideas for Introducing the Novel

- Give a brief book talk to arouse students' curiosity and interest (see **About the Novel** for ideas).

- Play or show a segment of an audio, film, or video version of the book or an interview with the writer.

- Present high-interest biographical information about the writer (see **About the Writer** in this Study Guide and the biographical sketch at the end of the HRW Library edition of this novel).

- Read aloud a passage from the novel that arouses your own interest, and elicit predictions, inferences, and speculations from students.

- Lead a focused class discussion or suggest activities that (1) draw on students' prior knowledge or (2) lead them to generate their own ideas about a significant topic or theme they will encounter in the novel (see **Before You Read).**

Reader's Log Starters

- When I began reading this book, I thought…
- My favorite part, so far, is…
- I predict that…
- I like the way the writer…
- I'd like to ask the writer…
- If I had written this book, I would have…
- This [character, incident, idea] reminds me of…
- This book made me think about…
- This book made me realize…

Questions for Reflection

- What was your favorite part of the book (and why)?

- If you could be one of the characters, who would it be (and why)?

- Would you or wouldn't you recommend this book to a friend (and why)?

- What is the most important thing about this book?

- Would you change the ending? If not, what makes it work? If yes, what changes would you make?

- If you could have a conversation with the writer, what would you say or ask?

Strategies for Inclusion

Each set of activities has been developed to meet special student interests, abilities, and learning styles. Because the questions and activities in this Study Guide are directed to the students, there are no labels to indicate the types of learners they target. However, in each Before You Read, Choices, *and* Novel Projects *page, you will find activities to meet the needs of*

- *less proficient readers*
- *students acquiring English*
- *advanced students*

The activities and projects have been prepared to accommodate these different learning styles:
- *auditory/musical*
- *interpersonal*
- *intrapersonal*
- *kinesthetic*
- *logical/mathematical*
- *verbal/linguistic*
- *visual/spatial*

Using the Study Guide Questions and Activities

Encourage students to adapt the suggestions given in the Study Guide to fit their own learning styles and interests. It is important to remember that students are full of surprises, and a question or activity that is challenging to an advanced student can also be handled successfully by students who are less proficient readers. The high interest level, flexibility, and variety of these questions and activities make them appropriate for a range of students.

Students should be encouraged to vary the types of activities they choose so that the same student is not regularly selecting writing or researching activities over those involving speaking, art, and performing, and vice versa. Individual and group work should also alternate, so that students have the opportunity to work on their own and as part of collaborative learning groups.

Working in Pairs and Groups

When students with varying abilities, cultural backgrounds, and learning styles work together, they can arrive at a deeper understanding of both the novel and one another.

Reading pairs can stop and check each other's responses to the novel at frequent intervals.

Students from different cultural groups can interview one another about how certain situations, character interactions, character motivations, and so on would be viewed in their home cultures.

Visualizing and Performing

Students who have difficulty with writing or with presenting their ideas orally can demonstrate their understanding of the novel in a variety of ways:

- making cluster diagrams or sketching their ideas

- creating tableaux showing where characters are in relation to one another during a scene, their poses or stances, and their facial expressions

- creating thought balloons with drawings or phrases that show what a character is thinking at a given moment

- drawing their own thoughts in thought balloons above a sketched self-portrait

- listing or drawing images that come to mind as they read or hear a certain section or passage of the novel

- making a comic-book version of the novel (with or without words)

- coming to class as a character in the novel

Assessment Options

Perhaps the most important goal of assessment is to inform instruction. As you monitor the degree to which your students understand and engage with the novel, you will naturally modify your instructional plan. The frequency and balance of class and small-group discussion, the time allowed for activities, and the extent to which direct teaching of reading skills and strategies, literary elements, or vocabulary is appropriate can all be planned on the basis of your ongoing assessment of your students' needs.

Several forms of assessment are particularly appropriate for work with the novel:

Observing and note taking Anecdotal records that reflect both the degree and the quality of students' participation in class and small-group discussions and activities will help you target areas in which coaching or intervention is appropriate. Because communication skills are such an integral part of working with the novel in a classroom setting, it is appropriate to evaluate the process of making meaning in this social context.

Involving yourself with dialogue journals and letters You may want to exchange notes with students instead of, or in addition to, encouraging them to keep reader's logs. A powerful advantage of this strategy is that at the same time you have the opportunity to evaluate students' responses, you can make a significant difference in the quality of the response. When students are aware that their comments are valued (and addressed to a real audience, an audience that writes back), they often wake up to the significance of what they are reading and begin to make stronger connections between the text and their own lives.

Agreeing on criteria for evaluation If evaluation is to be fair, it must be predictable. As students propose and plan an activity or project, collaborate with them to set up the criteria by which their work will be evaluated, and be consistent in applying only those criteria.

Encouraging self-evaluation and goal setting When students are partners with you in creating criteria for evaluation, they can apply those criteria to their own work. You might ask them to rate themselves on a simple scale of 1, 2, or 3 for each of the criteria and to arrive at an overall score. Students can then set goals based on self-evaluation.

Peer evaluation Students can participate in evaluating one another's demonstrations and presentations, basing their evaluations upon a previously established set of standards. Modeling a peer-evaluation session will help students learn this method, and a chart or checklist can guide peer discussion. Encourage students to be objective, sensitive, courteous, and constructive in their comments.

Keeping portfolios If you are in an environment where portfolios contain only carefully chosen samples of students' writing, you may want to introduce a second, "working," portfolio and negotiate grades with students after examining all or selected items from these portfolios.

Opportunities for Assessment

The suggestions in this Study Guide provide multiple opportunities for assessment across a range of skills:

- demonstrating reading comprehension
- keeping reader's logs
- listening and speaking
- working in groups—both discussion and activity-oriented
- planning, developing, and presenting a final project
- acquiring vocabulary
- taking tests

Questions for Self-evaluation and Goal Setting

- What are the three most important things I learned in my work with this novel?
- How will I follow up with these so that I remember them?
- What was the most difficult part of working with this novel?
- How did I deal with the difficulty, and what would I do differently?
- What two goals will I work toward in my [reading/writing/group work, etc.]?
- What steps will I take to achieve those goals?

Items for a "Working" Portfolio

- reading records
- drafts of written work and project plans
- audio- and videotapes of presentations
- notes on discussions
- reminders of cooperative projects, such as planning and discussion notes
- artwork
- objects and mementos connected with themes and topics in the novel
- other evidence of engagement with the book

For help with establishing and maintaining portfolio assessment, examine the **Portfolio Management System** *in* **Elements of Literature.**

About the Writer

Christopher Paul Curtis

More on Curtis

Beldo, Sarah. "Author Curtis to captivate Rackham audience tonight." *The Michigan Daily*, March 28, 1996. Available online at http://www.pub.umich.edu/daily/1996/mar/03-28-96/arts/curtis.author.feat.html A brief biocritical overview.

"Christopher Paul Curtis." *Bantam Doubleday Dell Books for Young Readers Teacher's Resource Center/authors + illustrators index.* Available online at http://www.bdd.com/bin/forums/teachers/curt.html   Biographical and autobiographical articles, with a link to a RealAudio message from the author.

Frederick, Heather Vogel. "Flying Starts." *Publishers Weekly*, December 18, 1995, pp. 28–29. An article on "debut" authors that leads off with a discussion of Curtis.

Lannon, Linnea. "First-time author finds niche on many 'best' lists for young adult readers." *Knight-Ridder/Tribune News Service*, December 27, 1995. The writing and publication of the Watsons' story, peppered with quotations from Curtis and his family.

A biography of Christopher Paul Curtis appears in **The Watsons Go to Birmingham—1963,** *HRW Library edition. You may wish to share this additional biographical information with your students.*

Christopher Paul Curtis grew up with parents who were strict, laying down rules that the children were expected to follow. His ideas for *The Watsons Go to Birmingham—1963* grew, in part, out of these childhood experiences. Some episodes in the novel were drawn from life, too. Like the fictional Byron, as a boy, Curtis played with matches. Desperate to end the play before disaster struck, his mother tried to burn his fingers with a match, but his younger sister kept blowing out the matches. Although some ideas and details came from Curtis's own life, most did not. The Watsons and other characters are a blend of many people, he says.

Curtis chose 1963 as the setting for his novel because he remembers the time so vividly. His father was active in the civil rights movement, which was then front-page news. In 1963, Curtis was about the same age as Kenny, the narrator of *The Watsons Go to Birmingham—1963.*

Curtis recalls that the creative challenge didn't end with writing the novel. Like all first-time novelists, he faced difficult odds to get his book published. Curtis attacked the problem by entering his novel in a contest sponsored by the publisher Delacorte. The novel didn't qualify for the contest, but Delacorte read it and decided to publish it anyway.

Since the publication of *The Watsons Go to Birmingham—1963,* Curtis has returned to the public library to complete a few more books he has in the works.

About the Novel

The Watsons Go to Birmingham—1963

Christopher Paul Curtis didn't write *The Watsons Go to Birmingham—1963* specifically as a novel for young people, but it has wrapped up many honors in that category.

CRITICAL COMMENT

This first novel has been almost universally praised by critics thus far. It rates high on many lists of recommended readings. Kermit Frazier, in *The New York Times Book Review,* gives Curtis thumbs up for "a marvelous debut, a fine novel about a solid and appealing family." *Publishers Weekly* comments that it evokes a full range of emotions and that "this exceptional first novel is certain to reverberate within the reader's psyche."

The two most commented-upon qualities of *The Watsons Go to Birmingham—1963* are the robust humor that weaves its way through the first half of the book and the incorporation of a real event—the bombing of the Sixteenth Street Baptist Church in Birmingham, Alabama. Curtis, who changed his original ending to include the bombing, commented that the idea came to him in such a roundabout manner that he could not prepare the reader for it with foreshadowing. Indeed, that "might have taken away from the impact," Curtis reasons.

The blending of humor with serious and tragic elements into one cohesive novel also caught reviewers' attention. Sarah Beldo observes in *The Michigan Daily* that one of Curtis's achievements is to retain the innocent voice of Kenny throughout the novel, from the humorous first chapters to the tragic and psychologically compelling final chapters. "[H]e never loses his believability," she says, "even when describing a child's reaction to a horrific event." A review in *The Horn Book Magazine* adds that "Curtis's control of his material is superb as he unconventionally shifts tone and mood, as he depicts the changing relationship between the two brothers, and as he incorporates a factual event into his fictional story." Cindy Darling Codell comments in the *School Library Journal* that "Curtis's ability to switch from fun and funky to pinpoint-accurate psychological imagery works unusually well."

Awards and Honors

Newbery Honor Book

Coretta Scott King Honor Book

ALA Best Book for Young Adults

ALA Notable Book

IRA Young Adults' Choice

Bank Street Child Study Association Children's Book Award

The New York Times Book Review Best Book

Publishers Weekly Best Book

The Horn Book Fanfare

Bulletin Blue Ribbon

Golden Kite Award for Fiction

For Listening

The Watsons Go to Birmingham—1963. Bantam Audio, 1996. Narrated by actor LeVar Burton.

Key Elements

Make a Connection

Call on volunteers to name some current events found in the news. If students were writing the story of this year in their lives, which of those events would be included? Why?

Plot

Chapters 1–3 It's frigid in Flint, Michigan, and the "Weird Watsons" decide to visit Aunt Cydney, who has a warm house. Kenny and Byron go out to scrape the ice off the car; instead of scraping, though, Byron kisses his image in the car mirror and his lips freeze to it. Momma yanks him from the mirror. At school, Kenny is teased frequently; he has a lazy eye and is smart—an unfortunate combination. Things improve when a new boy, Rufus, starts school and becomes the new target for ridicule. Rufus and Kenny become friends and often play together. One day Kenny forgets himself and laughs when someone pokes fun at Rufus and his brother. Rufus is offended, but the friendship is salvaged when Kenny's mother intervenes.

Chapters 4–7 Momma always bundles Kenny and Joey in mountains of clothing during the winter. Joey complains, but Byron assures her that people can freeze solid. Kenny has two pairs of gloves and gives Rufus the extra pair. When Kenny's gloves disappear, he learns that Larry Dunn has stolen them. Byron retrieves the gloves and gives Larry a hard time. A few days later, Momma catches Byron playing with matches. To teach Byron a lesson, she tries to burn his fingers with matches, but Joey saves him by blowing out the matches. Byron later learns that he can sign for food at the store, so he gets two bags of cookies. He hurls a cookie at a mourning dove and kills it. His response surprises Kenny. Next, Byron gets his hair conked. Dad responds by shaving Byron's head.

Chapters 8–11 Dad gets the family car, the Brown Bomber, ready for a long trip and adds one extravagant item: a car record player. Momma thinks that it is too expensive, but they all agree that it is great. Momma then announces that they are going to Alabama, where Byron will stay with Grandma Sands to stay out of trouble, at least for the summer. Although Momma has planned every step of the trip thoroughly, Dad decides to drive straight through. Kenny and most of the family sleep much of the way, although they do wake up to look at the night sky in the mountains and to feel the mountain air. When they arrive, Kenny is surprised both at Grandma Sands herself and at the effect she has on Byron.

Chapter 12–Epilogue When the children plan to go swimming, Grandma Sands warns them about whirlpools; Joey doesn't understand *whirlpool,* and Byron tells her it's *Wool Pooh,* Winnie-the-Pooh's evil twin. When Kenny goes swimming and nearly drowns, he believes that the Wool Pooh has tried to pull him under. Byron saves him. On Sunday, Joey goes to the Sunday school where a bomb later explodes. Kenny races to the church and fears that he sees Joey's shoe under the rubble. Again, he thinks he sees the Wool Pooh. Joey is safe, however, and the Watsons return to Flint. Kenny is unable to make sense of what he saw at the bombed church and is ashamed that he abandoned Joey to the Wool Pooh. He retreats to a secret hiding place behind the couch; Byron eventually helps him come to terms with what happened.

In the Epilogue, Curtis relates the bombing to the history of the civil rights movement.

Plot Structure Kenny faces **external conflicts** as he struggles with the teasing and tormenting both his brother and other students at school, especially Larry Dunn, inflict on him. He must also deal with **internal conflict,** most vividly in response to the church bombing. He is torn between the urge to rescue his sister and his fear of the Wool Pooh. With Byron's help, he works through the pain of this experience in the novel's denouement after the family has returned to Flint.

Theme

Students will see the following **themes,** or main ideas, developed in detail in *The Watsons Go to Birmingham—1963*.

The Importance of Family The "Weird Watsons" are a close-knit family whose members look after one another. Momma and Dad keep strict control over their children and demonstrate the joy of family life through humor, love, and everyday activities. They do what is necessary to protect their children, even when it requires "tough love"—as in sentencing Byron to a summer with Grandma Sands. Byron and Kenny go after each other constantly; but when either is in trouble, each stands up for the other. Joey constantly worries about her brothers and takes action when she can to protect them, as when she blows out matches to help Byron.

The Power of Prejudice This novel takes place during the early years of the civil rights movement, when African Americans were struggling to overcome racial discrimination. This theme is developed most clearly in the latter half of the novel, when the church in Birmingham is bombed. Not only is the church destroyed and four girls killed, but repercussions follow the Watsons back to Michigan.

Make a Connection

Ask students what the word *prejudice* means to them. Discuss the ways in which prejudice can influence people. How does it affect the way its victims think, feel, and act?

Connecting with Elements of Literature

You can use *The Watsons Go to Birmingham—1963* to extend students' examination of the themes and topics presented in *Elements of Literature.*

- Introductory Course: "Justice for All," Collection Five
- First Course: "Out Here on My Own," Collection One
- Second Course: "I Still Believe," Collection Five

Kenny is haunted by the violence, the racial hatred, and the shame he feels for abandoning his sister. His solace comes when Byron helps him realize that "things ain't never gonna be fair," and that "you just gotta understand that that's the way it is and keep on steppin'."

Although the bombing is the most vivid example of the power of prejudice, the theme is evident throughout the novel. In Chapter 3, Kenny's classmates make Rufus a victim of prejudice because of his country ways. Later, the Watsons plan their trip to Alabama carefully because of the risks for a black family traveling through the South in 1963.

Make a Connection

Call on volunteers to name ways in which brothers and sisters can have very distinct personalities. As students read, challenge them to keep a list of words and phrases that describe each of the three Watsons and help distinguish them as **characters.**

Characters

Students will meet the following **characters** in *The Watsons Go to Birmingham—1963*.

Kenny, the narrator, is ten years old, smart, and sensitive.

Byron is Kenny's thirteen-year-old brother. He loves adventures, harassing Kenny, and being "cool." His parents fear that he is at risk of becoming a juvenile delinquent.

Joetta, or Joey, is the youngest and yet in some ways the most mature of the three Watson children.

Dad is Daniel Watson. He works hard and has a strong sense of humor. He looks after his family carefully and tries to provide firm guidance for his children.

Momma is Wilona Watson. She is from Alabama and has never completely adapted to the cold Michigan winters. Momma is a careful planner and a strict parent.

Rufus Fry has recently arrived in Michigan from Arkansas. He becomes Kenny's close friend.

Grandma Sands, Wilona Watson's mother, lives in Birmingham.

Mr. Robert, who takes the boys fishing and tells hunting stories, is Grandma Sands' "dearest friend."

Setting

The opening chapters of *The Watsons Go to Birmingham—1963* take place in the winter and spring of 1963 in Flint, Michigan. In the later chapters, the Watsons travel by car to Birmingham, Alabama. In the final chapters, the family is again in Flint. The movement between the two settings helps underscore differences between the North and South and provides a structure for the novel's rising action, climax and denouement.

The time period is as important to the novel as the places where the action occurs. In 1963, the civil rights movement gained greater national attention—both for Dr. Martin Luther King, Jr.'s, inspiring "I Have a Dream" speech and for hate crimes such as the bombing of the Sixteenth Street Baptist Church. These events lend weight to the characters' actions and provide the novel's climax.

Point of View

The Watsons Go to Birmingham—1963 is narrated by Kenny Watson, using a **first-person point of view.** The narration reflects Kenny's innocence, limited experiences, love for his family, and childish concerns, fears, and attitudes. Readers experience Kenny's transition from an innocent child whose conflicts center on fitting in with his classmates to a young person discovering the power of evil.

Allusion

An **allusion** is a reference to someone or something from literature, history, religion, mythology, or another field that is familiar to many people. Allusions enrich the reading experience by providing, in just a few words, an additional layer of meaning and emotional content. For example, when Byron's lips are frozen to the car mirror, Joey alludes to "Nar-sissy." She's referring to Narcissus, a youth in Greek mythology who loves no one until he sees his own reflection in a pool. He remains there, pining after his own image until he dies.

The Watsons Go to Birmingham—1963 is rich in allusion. Here are two more examples:

• Chapter 7: "Yul Watson," the "long-lost son from Siam" alludes to actor Yul Brynner, who shaved his head for the role in the 1956 film *The King and I*.

• Chapter 11: The question *et tu, Brute?* is a Shakespearean allusion. The title character in *Julius Caesar* asks it when his friend Brutus betrays him by joining his assassins.

Make a Connection

Discuss the **first-person point of view,** emphasizing that the reader can know only what the narrator knows. Read a few lines of the novel to students. How would it be different if it were written from the **third-person limited point of view** or from an **omniscient point of view?**

A Literary Elements Worksheet that focuses on allusion appears on page 40 of this Study Guide.

Key Elements (continued) *The Watsons Go to Birmingham—1963*

*A **Literary Elements Worksheet** that focuses on atmosphere/mood appears on page 41 of this Study Guide.*

Atmosphere / Mood

One intriguing aspect of *The Watsons Go to Birmingham—1963* is the dramatic shift in **atmosphere** or **mood**—in other words, in "feeling"—after the Watsons reach Alabama. The atmosphere in Chapters 1–11 is humorous and lighthearted. Soon after the family reaches Alabama, however, the atmosphere becomes threatening.

Curtis creates atmosphere with **images** and language that convey particular feelings. Chapters 1–11 are filled with humorous images, like that of Joey stuffed into her layers of winter clothes, and humorous **dialogue,** as when the father displays his new record player. The images and dialogue of the final four chapters are more serious—the Wool Pooh, Kenny's hiding place, and Byron's conversation with Kenny in the bathroom, for example.

Make a Connection

Remind students that *The Watsons Go to Birmingham—1963* is both about a family and about the civil rights movement. Knowing this ahead of time, what **conflicts** might students predict that the family might face?

*A **Literary Elements Worksheet** that focuses on conflict appears on page 42 of this Study Guide.*

Conflict

Every **plot** is constructed around **conflict,** the struggle between opposing characters or opposing forces. It provides **motivation** for the **characters** and keeps the plot moving forward. The Watsons' story includes many **external conflicts**—conflicts between a character and an outside force. Examples include Byron's conflict with his parents over his hair and Kenny's conflict with Larry Dunn over the Maytag Wash. Other conflicts are **internal,** taking place within a character's mind. Examples include Kenny's conflict over how to resolve his quarrel with Rufus and over his fears relating to the violence that he witnessed in Birmingham.

Before You Read

Activities

BUILDING ON PRIOR KNOWLEDGE

Way Back When?

What do you know about the early 1960s? Meet with a group and brainstorm about this time period. What have you learned about these years from history class or from television and films? What was happening in politics, war, and civil rights? What movies and television programs were popular then? What were the cars like? How did people dress? Make a list of ideas. To make sure you're on the right track, check with a parent or other adult who lived during that time. Then share your ideas with other students in a class discussion.

EXPLORING THEMES

Bully for You!

What is a *bully?* You will meet some in this novel. Before you read, however, think about bullies that you have known. Then meet with some classmates to talk about ways of dealing with bullies. For example, is running away always a good idea? What about fighting back or trying to get help? Are there ways to turn a bully into a friend? As a group, choose the three ideas you like best and present them to the class. As a class, discuss each idea and vote for the top three "bully busters." Then watch to see how characters in *The Watsons Go to Birmingham— 1963* deal with bullies.

MAKING PERSONAL CONNECTIONS

On the Road Again

Have you ever taken a long car trip? What was the traveling like? How different from home was the place you visited? How did you feel about going home? Write or draw to express your feelings about that experience. If you never have had such a trip, use writing or drawing to express your ideas about what it might be like. Keep your writing or artwork handy as you read to compare your trip with the one in this novel.

DISCUSSING

What Rights Are Missing?

There are many ways in which people's rights are limited or even taken away. Laws can be used to take away rights, but there are other ways (some of which happen in spite of laws). For example, a neighborhood bully can limit your right to use the park. Lack of an elevator can prevent a disabled person from using the second floor of a public library. With a group, list and discuss other ways in which the rights of individuals can be limited. Then do some brainstorming. How might people overcome these restrictions?

Novel Notes

Use **Novel Notes, Issue 1**

- to find out more about some of the topics and themes in *The Watsons Go to Birmingham—1963*
- to get ideas for writing activities and other projects that will take you deeper into the book

Making Meanings

First Thoughts

1. Both Kenny and Rufus get unpleasant attention from other students at school. With which **character** do you sympathize more—Kenny or Rufus? Explain.

Shaping Interpretations

2. What is Byron like? What **motivation,** or guiding reason, causes him to act the way he does?

3. When he finds that Byron's lips have frozen to the mirror, Dad laughs until he cries. Why isn't he more concerned?

4. **Figures of speech** are brief **descriptions** that are not meant to be taken literally. Exaggeration is one kind of figure of speech. Give three examples of exaggeration from Chapters 1–3 and explain the meaning of each one.

5. How does the game in "The World's Greatest Dinosaur War Ever" help you understand Kenny better?

6. Kenny's wish for a "personal saver" seems to come true when he meets Rufus. Then things take an unexpected turn. At the end of Chapter 3, is Rufus a "personal saver" for Kenny? Explain.

Connecting with the Text

7. Kenny is taken to Byron's class so that the older students can hear "how well this young man reads." Kenny does not like the experience. How would you feel in his shoes? Why?

Extending the Text

8. Suppose that Kenny were big, strong, and tough like Byron. How might he have reacted to the way that other students were treating Rufus? Explain.

Challenging the Text

9. Is the **dialogue** in this novel realistic? Give examples from Chapters 1–3 to support your answer.

Choices: Building Your Portfolio

COOPERATIVE LEARNING

What a Family!

Talk about Chapters 1–3 with two classmates. In particular, discuss the **characters** of Kenny, Byron, Momma, and Dad. Is this a typical family? Think about the ways in which they behave and respond to one another. Even if things don't always go smoothly for them, are they happy? How can you tell? List ways in which these four Watsons illustrate the novel's **theme** of "The Importance of Family."

VOCABULARY BUILDING

Talk Talk

Much of *The Watsons Go to Birmingham—1963* is written in informal English. It's filled with slang, idioms, **dialect,** and regional expressions. Make a list of words and phrases that are unusual or difficult to understand. Use a dictionary and talk to other students and to your teacher to learn the meaning of these terms. Create a dictionary of the new terms. You may want to keep adding to your personal dictionary as you continue reading this novel.

ART

A Scenic View

With three classmates, choose four key **scenes** from Chapters 1-3. Divide the scenes among you. Working on your own, decide how you can best illustrate the scene and create artwork that gets your idea across. Then, meet with the other members of your group and discuss your drawings. Explain why you chose to illustrate your scene as you did. Then, as a group, present your illustrations to the class.

CREATIVE WRITING

I Remember When . . .

Kenny tells some entertaining stories about growing up with Byron. Write a short story less than a page long about Byron from Kenny's point of view. (Remember: Kenny is ten years old, and he is good at including dialogue. Try to make your "Kenny" like the "Kenny" in the novel.) After you finish, read your story to a group of classmates. If several students in your class work on this activity, you might gather the stories into a class anthology.

Consider This . . .

I guess I should have told Momma that I really appreciated her helping me get my friend back but I didn't have to. I was pretty sure she already knew.

How did Momma do this favor for Kenny? What makes Kenny think that she knows how much he appreciates it?

Writing Follow-up: Reflecting ━━━━━ ■

Think about a favor that a parent or other adult has done for you. How did you express your appreciation?

Novel Notes

Use **Novel Notes, Issue 2**

- to find out more about some of the topics and themes in Chapters 1–3
- to get ideas for writing activities and other projects related to *The Watsons Go to Birmingham—1963*

Making Meanings

First Thoughts

1. Would you want Byron for a brother? Why or why not?

Shaping Interpretations

2. When Byron bullies Larry Dunn, the other students gather around to enjoy the show. Kenny leaves, however. What does this action tell you about his personality and values?

3. Why does Byron come into **conflict** with Momma over the idea that the family might be eating welfare food?

4. Why are Momma and Dad so displeased with Byron when he gets a conk?

5. Which **scene** did you find the most humorous? Explain.

6. Which of the three children—Kenny, Byron, or Joey—seems to be the most mature **character?** Explain.

Connecting with the Text

7. Momma decides to burn Byron's fingers to teach him a lesson about playing with matches. What is your opinion of this method of discipline?

Extending the Text

8. What discipline techniques can you think of that might help Byron stay out of trouble? Why would these methods work for him?

Challenging the Text

9. When Momma tries to burn Byron's fingers, Joetta blows out match after match. Joey is only a kindergartener—but she stops the punishment. In your opinion, would most kindergarteners react this way, or is Joey unusual? Explain your answer.

Choices: Building Your Portfolio

COOPERATIVE LEARNING

On the Spot

Get together with two classmates and make up a list of questions that you would like to ask Christopher Paul Curtis about *The Watsons Go to Birmingham—1963*. From this list, choose the questions you would most like to have answered. Then, ask these questions in a short letter to the author in care of the publisher. If you get a quick response, share it with the other members of your group or the whole class.

CROSSING THE CURRICULUM: MUSIC

Watsong

The Watsons love music, so write a song about one of the events in this section of their story. (These titles might give you some ideas: "Oh, Those Winter Clothes," "Larry Dunn, Larry Dunn," "Don't You Light That Match," or "The Ballad of the Swedish Cremes.") You may use the tune of a song that you know, but make the lyrics your own. After you have practiced, perform your song for the class. If you like, invite classmates to join in the performance.

CREATIVE WRITING

Showdown!

Confronting a bully like Larry Dunn is a story idea guaranteed to hold a reader's interest. On your own or with a partner, write a short story with a different **setting** about someone who is forced into a showdown with a bully. Your story may be only a few paragraphs, but it should have a clear beginning, middle, and end. Try to get across some of the feelings that Larry Dunn inspired in you. Then share your story with the class.

CARTOONING

Comic Relief

Choose a memorable scene from this section of the novel and create a comic strip of it. Your comic strip should be four panels long and include both illustrations and dialogue. You may want to enhance it with color, then share it with the class.

Consider This . . .

Leave it to Daddy Cool to kill a bird, then give it a funeral. Leave it to Daddy Cool to torture human kids at school all day long and never have his conscience bother him but to feel sorry for a stupid little grayish brown bird.

What does Kenny think about his brother at this moment? How can you explain Byron's behavior?

Writing Follow-up: Comparing / Contrasting

Byron shows two distinct sides of his personality in this section of the novel. Compare and contrast these two sides. Which side does Byron show most often?

Novel Notes

Use **Novel Notes, Issue 3**

- to find out more about some of the topics and themes in Chapters 4–7
- to get ideas for writing activities and other projects related to *The Watsons Go to Birmingham—1963*.

The Watsons Go to Birmingham—1963

Making Meanings

First Thoughts

1. Would you want to go along on the Watsons' car trip? Why or why not?

Shaping Interpretations

2. In Chapter 8, the **dialogue** between Dad and Kenny in the bathroom doesn't add anything to the plot of the novel. Why do you think Curtis included it?

3. Kenny asks Dad if it is really necessary to leave Byron in Alabama. In your own words, explain the reasons Dad gives Kenny.

4. Before the trip, Byron brags to Buphead that he will not say a single word during the trip. When the family starts out, however, he talks right away. Explain his behavior.

5. Why does Momma become frightened when they stop on the mountain?

6. What does Kenny mean when he uses this **figure of speech** to describe Grandma Sands and Byron: "instead of Dracula and Frankenstein it was like Dracula and a giraffe, and Byron was all neck"?

Connecting with the Text

7. Think about a time when you met someone you had heard about and imagined. Was this person what you expected? Explain.

Extending the Text

8. Byron's behavior quickly changes when he meets Grandma Sands. What qualities do some people (like Grandma Sands) have that inspire people to respect and obey them?

Challenging the Text

9. Think about the story of Mrs. Davidson and the angel. In your opinion, is this story important to the **plot** of the novel, or is it an interruption? Explain your answer.

The Watsons Go to Birmingham—1963

Choices: Building Your Portfolio

Topic Pick

With four or five classmates, choose one of the topics developed in *The Watsons Go to Birmingham—1963*. (Examples include family, life at school, discipline, friendship, prejudice, and grieving.) Take turns identifying and explaining an event or action in this section that seems to say something about the topic you have chosen. When you have discussed several episodes that illustrate one topic, choose another topic to explore.

Hit the Road, Jack

The Watsons travel from Flint, Michigan, to Birmingham, Alabama. Travel with them by creating a map of their route; show the states and major cities along the way. Make an educated guess about the site of the mountain where they stopped. Figure out the total distance and some of the distances between cities. Finally, estimate how long the trip would take at today's speed limits.

Car Tunes

Dad buys the Ultra-Glide so that the Watsons can enjoy their own music as they travel. Skim this part of their story, listing the songs, musicians, and types of music mentioned. Find recordings of some of these songs, or gather some facts about the music and musicians; then prepare a presentation for your class.

Starry, Starry Night

When the Watsons stop on the mountain, they see what Kenny calls a "star explosion"—a sky filled with stars. The **description** of that mountaintop and of the drive down the mountain is almost poetic, for it includes **similes** and other poetic devices. Re-read the description. Have you ever experienced a place that struck you as beautiful? Write a **poem** about it and consider sharing it with your class.

Consider This . . .

"Byron is getting old enough to have to understand that his time for playing is running out fast, he's got to realize the world doesn't have a lot of jokes waiting for him. He's got to be ready."

Dad is explaining to Kenny why Byron must go to Alabama. What do you think of Dad's reasoning?

Writing Follow-up: Explaining ■

How can a young person "get ready" for the adult world? Explain in detail three ways to prepare for this transition.

Novel Notes

Use **Novel Notes, Issue 4**

- to find out more about some of the topics and themes in Chapters 8–11
- to get ideas for writing activities and other projects related to *The Watsons Go to Birmingham—1963*

The Watsons Go to Birmingham—1963

Making Meanings

a. What happens at Collier's Landing?

b. According to Byron, what is the Wool Pooh?

c. What happens at the church? What happens to Joey there?

d. Why does Kenny stay at the World-Famous Watson Pet Hospital? Why does he leave?

First Thoughts

1. Respond to this part of the novel by completing these sentences.

   • When Kenny walked into the lake, I thought . . .
   • When Joey came to Kenny after the bombing, I thought . . .
   • When Byron talked to Kenny in the bathroom, I thought . . .

Shaping Interpretations

2. Why is it Kenny, not Byron, who decides to go to Collier's Landing?

3. At the bombed church, Kenny sees two girls lying in the grass, one wearing a red dress, the other in blue. Kenny thinks that if Joey were next to them, "their dresses would make the red, white and blue of the American flag." What do you think of this **imagery**? Why do you think the author included it?

4. Who motions to Joey to follow him and leave the church?

5. In your opinion, has seeing all that Kenny has gone through affected Byron? How can you tell?

6. Byron doesn't believe in unseen powers. Kenny does. Whose opinion do you think the novel supports?

Connecting with the Text

7. Byron plants the idea of the Wool Pooh in Kenny's mind, and Kenny sees the creature. Has anyone ever tricked you into believing something that later proved to be imaginary? Explain.

Extending the Text

8. The **setting** is 1963. Could the events in Birmingham take place today? Explain your answer.

Challenging the Text

9. Could the Epilogue have served as the book's prologue instead? Where would it be more effective—at the beginning or end of the novel? Why?

The Watsons Go to Birmingham—1963

Choices: Building Your Portfolio

A *Watsons* Quiz

Form a group to discuss one of the four sections of *The Watsons Go to Birmingham—1963*. In your group, write five questions about **characters, plot** details, **themes** of the novel, its **setting,** and so on. Write each question and its answer on an index card—a total of five cards. With your teacher's help, gather the cards and organize the class into two teams. The teacher or a student moderator can read each question aloud and keep score.

Just Like Me?

How well do you know yourself? One way to find out is to compare yourself to a fictional **character.** Choose a character from this book. On a sheet of paper, make two columns. In the left-hand column, list ways in which you think you are similar to that character in your thoughts, speech, and behavior. In the right-hand column, list ways in which you think that you are different from that character.

Birmingham Elegy

An **elegy** is a thoughtful poem in remembrance of someone who has died. Write an elegy for the four young girls who died in the bombing of the Birmingham church. Use what you have learned from the novel about the situation and the events that surrounded these girls and took their lives. Share your poem by reading it aloud or posting it on a class bulletin board.

Consider This . . .

"Kenny, things ain't ever going to be fair. . . . How's it fair that even though the cops down there might know who did it nothing will probably ever happen to those men? It ain't. But you just gotta understand that that's the way it is and keep on steppin'."

Byron is sharing some hard wisdom—something that perhaps he has just learned himself—with younger brother Kenny. Is it good advice?

Writing Follow-up: Reflecting ────■

Has there ever been a time when you had to just "keep on steppin'"? What did you learn from the experience?

Novel Notes

Use **Novel Notes, Issue 5**

- to find out more about some of the topics and themes in Chapter 12–Epilogue
- to get ideas for writing activities and other projects related to *The Watsons Go to Birmingham—1963*

The Watsons Go to Birmingham—1963

Cross-Curricular Connections

Civil Rights Time Line

The civil rights movement was going strong in 1963. Major events had already occurred; more were soon to follow. Do some research into the movement. Use the information that you find to create a time line of civil rights activities from the early 1950s to the present. You might enhance it with illustrations and display it in class or elsewhere in school.

Reflection

Ten-year-old Kenny would be a mature adult today. What might he think now about the experiences the novel describes? As the adult Kenny, reflect on what you experienced, how you dealt with it, and what place you and your family have in American history. Your reflection may be in the form of a letter, a journal entry, or any other appropriate form, and you may want to include a hint at what Kenny is doing now.

Civil Rights Movement in Pictures

Search for photographs that show the history of the civil rights movement. Look at the original newspaper and magazine reports of events when they occurred. You might also find some historic photographs that you can download from the Internet. Photocopy the pictures from your print resources. Then, use your imagination to find a way to display them. You might organize them as a photo essay that would appear in a magazine, or use them to illustrate biographies of civil rights leaders.

Movie Poster

Imagine that *The Watsons Go to Birmingham—1963* is being made into a movie. You have been hired to create a poster to promote the film. Decide which aspect of the novel you want to highlight and choose a fitting scene. Illustrate the scene as it might appear in the movie. Remember to give it a memorable slogan and to list the major stars.

Multimedia and Internet Connections

NOTE: *Check with your teacher about school policies on accessing Internet sites. If a Web site named here is not available, use key words to locate a similar site.*

JOURNALISM: TELEVISION

Live from the Scene

Imagine that you and several of your classmates make up a Birmingham television news crew. You're on the scene minutes after the bomb explodes in the church. Prepare a news broadcast of events as they unfold. You'll want to interview bystanders, survivors, the police, and firefighters. Prepare for the broadcast by investigating the September 15, 1963, bombing of the Sixteenth Street Baptist Church in Birmingham. (Refer to these Connections: "Schoolgirls Killed in Bombing," on page 227 of the text, and "Alabama Burning," on page 232.) Videotape your broadcast and share it with your class.

SOUNDTRACK: MUSIC

A Sound Idea

If *The Watsons Go to Birmingham—1963* were a film, what would its soundtrack be like? Think about the contrast between Michigan and Alabama as expressed in music on the Ultra-Glide and on the car radio. Think, too, about the songs that were part of the civil rights movement, such as "We Shall Overcome." Then, choose two or three pieces of music that could be part of a soundtrack for the film. Try to include at least two different kinds of music. As you share your choices with the class, explain how you think each one represents various **characters,** various events in the **plot,** or various **themes** of the novel.

RESEARCH: INTERNET

Is the Violence Over?

The story of the bombing of the church in Birmingham is based on a real event. That was not the first or the last time that churches have been targets of violence. Use the Internet to investigate more recent incidents of violence toward churches. Start with a keyword search of *church burnings.* Share your findings in a written summary or class discussion.

WRITING: INTERNET

Review Response

Look up *The Watsons Go to Birmingham—1963* at the Amazon.com bookstore Web site:

http://www.amazon.com

There you will find comments about the novel; some come from critics and others are from readers like you. Choose one comment and write a response to it. Explain why you agree or disagree with the comment. Use details from the novel to support your ideas. Help your teacher prepare a bulletin-board display on which you and your classmates can post the Web site comments and your responses.

MOVIE MAKING: VIDEO

See You in the Movies!

If you share Byron's interest in making movies, turn one of your creative ideas into a short (five minutes or less) video appropriate for classroom viewing. You may need to recruit a few other students to help out, and if you have never used your school's video equipment, you should ask your teacher how it works.

Exploring the Connections

Making Meanings

Childtimes

Novel Notes
See **Issue 6**

1. Which of the **settings** that Greenfield and Little describe appeals more to you? Why?

2. Why do the writers tell about all the vendors?

3. The **tone** of a piece of writing is the writer's attitude toward his or her subject. How would you describe the tone that Greenfield uses in speaking about the city where she grew up?

READING CHECK

a. What two "cities" within Washington, D.C., do Greenfield and Little describe?

b. Name two examples of segregation mentioned by Greenfield and Little.

c. Why do Greenfield and her family go to Parmele?

4. Compare the trip to Parmele taken by Greenfield's family with the Watsons' trip to Birmingham.

5. This story is a **memoir,** an account of Greenfield's own life. How does knowing that the story is **nonfiction** affect your response to it?

Grown-ups Always Ask

1. Based on your own family or other families you know, do you think the relationship described in this poem is realistic? Explain.

READING CHECK

According to the **speaker,** what is the important thing to know about having a fight with your brother and sister?

2. According to the speaker, children fight for "any reason or no reason." How would you explain the difference between these two reasons?

Novel Notes
See **Issue 6**

3. What lesson about brothers and sisters does this poem offer?

4. How is the speaker's relationship with her brothers and sisters like the relationship among Kenny, Byron, and Joey?

5. Do you think that the speaker would encourage children to fight with their brothers and sisters? Explain.

Exploring the Connections (continued)

Making Meanings

Two Interviews

Novel Notes
See ***Issue 7***

1. What do you think of the civil rights actions taken by Bernice Reagon and Walter Fauntroy? Explain your response.

2. What does Walter Fauntroy mean when he says, "Birmingham pricked this country's conscience"?

READING CHECK

a. How did Bernice Reagon overcome her fear?

b. How did Bull Connor bring national attention to the civil rights movement?

3. How has Fauntroy's work as a minister encouraged him to be a civil rights activist?

4. What connections do you see between these two interviews and *The Watsons Go to Birmingham—1963?*

5. Bernice Reagon says that singing gave her and the people around her the courage to participate in civil rights demonstrations. How does singing make you feel? Explain.

Schoolgirls Killed in Bombing

1. What feelings or ideas did you have after reading about the bombing of the church? Explain.

READING CHECK

Describe the situation at the Sixteenth Street Baptist Church just before the bomb exploded.

Novel Notes
See ***Issue 7***

2. Martin Luther King, Jr., said to the mourners that the "innocent blood of these little girls may well serve as the redemptive force." In your opinion, was he correct? Explain.

3. Why do you think it took 14 years before anyone was charged with the bombing?

4. Kenny was so deeply affected by his experience at the church that he stayed in the World-Famous Watson Pet Hospital for days after returning home. How does "Schoolgirls Killed in Bombing" help you understand Kenny's emotions?

Making Meanings

Novel Notes
See *Issue 7*

1. What thoughts and emotions do you have after reading this poem? Give details from the poem to support your response.

2. Why does the poet echo the first line twice later in the poem?

3. What do you think is "the breeze / As yet unfelt"?

4. How does the speaker's response to the tragedy differ from Kenny's?

5. In your opinion, have the hopes that the speaker expresses at the end of the poem been achieved? Why or why not?

> **READING CHECK**
>
> **a.** Who are the little girls who "never came back home"?
>
> **b.** What is the "Birmingham-on-Sunday wall"?

Alabama Burning

1. Does this article make you want to see the film? Why or why not?

2. When Spike Lee first asked Chris McNair if he could make the film, McNair turned him down because McNair didn't trust anyone. Why do you think that McNair was so distrustful?

> **READING CHECK**
>
> **a.** Describe the film that Spike Lee made.
>
> **b.** Why did Chris McNair give Lee permission to make the film?

Novel Notes
See *Issue 7*

3. Lee and McNair both say that the story of the bombing is important and needs to be told. Do you agree? Why?

4. How well do you think that *The Watsons Go to Birmingham—1963* helps people understand the events in Birmingham in 1963? Explain.

5. McNair makes a connection between the bombing in Birmingham and the more recent Oklahoma City bombing. Do you agree that there is a connection between violent events such as these? Explain.

Novel Notes

Introducing *The Watsons Go to Birmingham—1963*

SNAPSHOTS OF A YEAR: 1963

May 12: President John F. Kennedy sends federal **troops to Alabama** to protect citizens from violence between whites opposing school integration and blacks seeking equal rights.

June 15: Civil rights leader **Medgar Evers is murdered** at his home.

August 28: Martin Luther King, Jr., gives his **"I Have a Dream"** speech in front of the Lincoln Memorial in Washington, D.C.

November 22: President John F. **Kennedy is assassinated** during a motorcade procession in Dallas, Texas.

FOR YOUR READER'S LOG

What was it like to live in 1963? If you know someone who remembers this time, ask him or her about it and write down his or her comments in your Reader's Log. Then, as you read, contrast these comments with the picture of '60s life given in the novel.

⌛ TIME CAPSULE FROM THE 1960s OPENED ⌛

January 1, 2063: A crowd looked on in amazement as officials opened a time capsule filled with artifacts of the 1960s. The first item extracted was a primitive wooden skateboard. Though a member of the crowd attempted to ride this item, he was unable to execute a sharp turn on it, and the noise made by the hard wheels annoyed many.

Officials next pulled a disposable diaper from the capsule. The plain white throwaway item was reportedly introduced in 1961 as an alternative to the cloth diaper. Next, a unique piece of clothing appeared——a pair of bell-bottom jeans. Finally, a color television emerged. To the delight of the crowd, when the set was plugged in, it still worked and received only television shows popular during the '60s. They included *The Andy Griffith Show, Dr. Kildare, The Flintstones, The Beverly Hillbillies,* and *The Twilight Zone.*

The Word PLACE

Hey, all you sixties guys and gals! Take a little quiz to see whether you're hip or square. Match the latest lingo to the definitions.

1. any cool guy you happen to be talking to
2. very good and satisfying
3. hair treated with a chemical to straighten it
4. to understand or "get it"
5. a name used to address any boy or man
6. to assault or mug someone
7. foolish, nonsense
8. a phonograph record
9. a young, inexperienced boy
10. an old-fashioned person

The Lingo

a. jive	**f.** platter
b. Jack	**g.** punk
c. Daddy-o	**h.** conk
d. cool	**i.** dig
e. square	**j.** jack up

(Answers: 1. c; 2. d; 3. h; 4. i; 5. b; 6. j; 7. a; 8. f; 9. g; 10. e.)

Novel Notes

Issue 2

The Watsons Go to Birmingham—1963 Chapters 1–3

COME TO BIRMINGHAM FOR THE WINTER!

Tired of cold? Come to Birmingham, Alabama, where the average January high temperature is 56 degrees and the average low is an above-freezing 35. No danger of frostbite in Birmingham. The city affords many recreational opportunities, with the Talladega National Forest and the Coosa River less than an hour's drive to the east. Birmingham is also known for the Ruffner Mountain Nature Center, and Oak Mountain State Park. Visit the Birmingham Zoo or one of the city's famous steel refineries. If you come in July, be prepared for temperatures of 90 degrees and above. (Don't come in July!)

FOR YOUR READER'S LOG

Have you ever had anyone make fun of you? Have you ever made fun of someone else? In your Reader's Log, write about how you felt when you were teased. Compare your feelings to those of Kenny and Rufus as you read this section.

Why Not Spend This Summer in Flint?

Flint, Michigan, is not only a manufacturing city. Just forty miles south of Saginaw Bay on Lake Huron, Flint is a "City of Fun" in the summer. Walk the banks of the Flint River or watch the ducks on Thread Lake. Visit an automotive manufacturing plant in the afternoon and take in a symphony concert at night. Come to Flint! Average Fahrenheit temperatures in July include a high of 84 and a low of 63—quite a contrast to the average high of 32 degrees in January. (Don't come to Flint in the wintertime!)

ASK the Professor

Dear Dr. I. Knoweverything,

I have a new friend. There is just one thing about him that puzzles me. One of his eyes seems to be looking away from me when I talk to him. It doesn't bother me, but I don't know him well enough to ask him why his eye acts this way. Can you tell me?

—Looking Out for My Friend

Dear Looking,

Your friend has a condition called amblyopia (sometimes called "lazy eye"). Amblyopia results from some prior condition which gives supremacy to one eye over the other. The brain receives two nonidentical signals rather than the normal identical signals. Since the conflict between the signals is unpleasant for the brain, it ignores one of them, and that eye becomes a lazy eye. Both eyes work, but the brain does not register the visual input from the nontracking eye. This condition usually occurs during childhood; most cases can be cured using eyeglasses with a frosted or covered lens over the good eye or with surgery or vision exercises. The causes of lazy eye range from cataracts to a hairstyle that constantly covers one eye.

Novel Notes

Issue 3

The Watsons Go to Birmingham—1963 Chapters 4–7

A REPORT FROM THE LINGUISTIC COMMUNITY

Research Finds that Everyone Speaks a Dialect

A recently released bulletin from the *Novel Notes* Language Staff indicates that everyone speaks a dialect. The ingredients of a dialect are distinct vocabulary, pronunciation, and grammar; if your language has all of those things (and everyone's does), then you speak a dialect. If you don't think you speak a dialect, it's just because everyone around you speaks the same one. People who grow up in one area and then move to a different area as adults often retain their childhood dialect. Even though it's more noticeable when it's unusual, the fact is that everyone speaks a dialect, y'all he-uh what I'm a-sayin'?

FOR YOUR READER'S LOG

Do brothers and sisters have a responsibility to stand by each other? How would Kenny answer that? Byron? Joey? Think about what their answers might be as you read this section. Write down your thoughts in your Reader's Log.

The Word PLACE

Malapropisms

When Joey complains about being "the laughing sock of the morning kindergarten," she is using a *malapropism*. Malapropisms are funny because the speaker unintentionally misuses a word similar to the one he or she means to use (like Joey saying "laughing sock" when she means "laughing stock").

The term *malapropism* comes from Mrs. Malaprop, a character in Richard Sheridan's 1775 play *The Rivals* who often says *almost* the right word. Here are a few more examples of malapropisms:

There weren't any instruments, so she sang Acapulco. (instead of *a cappella*)

After surgery, patients need to stay in expensive care. (instead of *intensive care*)

Moses brought the Ten Commandments down from Mount Cyanide. (instead of *Mount Sinai*)

MEDICAL ALERT!

Frostbite Danger Next 24 Hours

Medical authorities have issued a frostbite warning for the next twenty-four hours. Residents of this area are urged to be cautious about venturing out into the cold without adequate clothing. People are being asked to watch children carefully to be sure that they do not become exposed to temperatures below 32 degrees Fahrenheit. Authorities also advise checking on elderly persons living alone, since they are especially susceptible to frostbite, particularly in the event of a home-heating-system failure.

Frostbite occurs when the flesh freezes solid; it always results in damage to tissue and frequently kills tissue under the skin. Don't think it can only happen to Arctic explorers! Watch for further details as weather conditions develop.

Novel Notes

The Watsons Go to Birmingham—1963 Chapters 8–11

Buy Two, Get a Third Record Free!

Special Groovy Tunes offer this Friday and Saturday only: buy any two 45s at the regular low price of $1.00 and get one more absolutely free. Get all the biggest hits of '63: Bobby Vinton's "Blue Velvet"; "Surfin' USA" by the Beach Boys; "He's So Fine" from the Chiffons. Take home a stack of 45s to keep your changer pumping sound for hours. Also get Golden Oldies like "Yakety Yak," the 1958 hit by the Coasters. Sing along with these lyrics:

Yakety Yak

Take out the papers and the trash
Or you don't get no spendin' cash
If you don't scrub that kitchen floor
You ain't gonna rock and roll no more
Yakety yak (don't talk back)

Just finish cleanin' up your room
Let's see that dust fly with that broom
Get all that garbage out of sight
Or you don't go out Friday night
Yakety yak (don't talk back)

You just put on your coat and hat
And walk yourself to the laundrymat
And when you finish doing that
Bring in the dog and put out the cat
Yakety yak (don't talk back)

Don't you give me no dirty looks
Your father's hip; he knows what cooks
Just tell your hoodlum friend outside
You ain't got time to take a ride
Yakety yak (don't talk back)

(Repeat and fade:)
Yakety yak, yakety yak

FOR YOUR READER'S LOG

Have you ever been on a long road trip? Traveling by car, especially when you're traveling with someone else along, is always an experience—sometimes good, sometimes awful. Write about your own experience with car travel and compare this with the Watsons' trip down I-75.

ASK the Professor

Dear Dr. I. Knoweverything,
I am the mother of a ten-year-old boy who has always been a good child and done well in school. Lately, however, he has started to show signs of a distorted mind. He is starting to see things! Or maybe I should say he is starting to see things that aren't there in place of things that are there. For instance, yesterday we drove into the gas station to get gas and he said the pump looked like "a deformed, evil, one-armed space robot." Where did he get that idea? I looked for a robot and I am sure there was none in sight. I am starting to worry.

— **Very Literal in Lexington**

Dear Literal,
No worries about your son. He is actually showing signs of intelligence. He is noticing relationships between what he sees and what he imagines. The example you cite is called a simile. I might say that someone who understands this sort of thing is "as sharp as a tack." That's just another example. I don't mean that these people hang around bulletin boards or turn sneakers into tap shoes; I just mean they're pretty clever. Listen to your son. He is obviously as smart as a whip, language-wise.

Lyrics to "Yakety Yak," written by Jerry Leiber and Mike Stoller. Copyright © 1958 by Jerry Leiber and Mike Stoller. Reprinted by permission of *Leiber and Stoller Music.*

Novel Notes

The Watsons Go to Birmingham—1963 Chapter 12–Epilogue

Church Bombing Related to Court-ordered Desegregation

Someone planted a bomb in the Sixteenth Street Baptist Church of Birmingham, Alabama, on September 15, 1963. When the bomb exploded, it killed four girls and injured many more people. News of the bombing led to street violence in the city, during which two African American boys were shot to death.

The bombing and the fighting that followed were related to racial tensions in Birmingham resulting from enforcement of a federal law requiring that schools and other public facilities be desegregated. Governor George Wallace opposed this law and ordered local police to prevent high schools from opening so that blacks and whites would not integrate. On September 29, 1963, President Kennedy used federal troops to force the opening and integration of the schools.

FOR YOUR READER'S LOG

In the final section of the novel, the Watsons witness a tragedy. Because Kenny is the narrator, we understand his feelings best. What do you think the other characters are feeling? Choose one character besides Kenny and write about how this character's feelings about the tragic events the family experiences might differ from Kenny's.

WHIRLPOOL TRIVIA

Did you know . . .

- that whirlpools, while dangerous to swimmers, can also threaten boats?
- that three of the most famous whirlpools in the world are the whirlpool below Niagara Falls, the Maelstrom off the coast of Norway, and the Charybdis between Sicily and Italy?
- that the Charybdis whirlpool and the treacherous rocks near it are immortalized in *The Odyssey* as Scylla and Charybdis—two monsters that Odysseus and his crew must sail between?
- that whirlpools can be caused by the meeting of currents coming from opposite directions or by winds blowing against the current?

ASK the Professor

Dear Dr. I. Knoweverything,

I recently read a book that refers to "Jim Crow laws." What are these? What do they have to do with me?

—James T. Crow

Dear Mr. Crow,

Many people who share your name may not realize its historical significance. These laws, which date back to the 1800s, made it illegal for blacks and whites to share public facilities. They had to use separate schools, theaters, buses, and so forth. This began to change when the Supreme Court declared in *Brown v. Board of Education* that "separate but equal" educational facilities were not legal. Although the law changed, many people's attitudes did not. Some states refused to accept desegregation, and a period of violence followed.

Novel Notes

The Watsons Go to Birmingham—1963 Connections

✴ NOVEL NOTES PROFILE ✴

Name: Eloise Greenfield

Notable work: Coauthor of *Childtimes: A Three-Generation Memoir* and narrator of "Childtimes"

Tough times: She spent years sending her writing to publishers and getting rejections back.

Happy accident: After the beginning of the civil rights movement, people suddenly wanted to read about African American children. This resulted in a demand for writing such as Greenfield's.

Publication history: 34 books of poetry, short stories, and biographies

On the black experience: "It is necessary for Black children to have a true knowledge of their past and present, in order that they may develop an informed sense of direction for their future."[1]

On the human spirit: "Children need to be aware of the spirit within them, that it's something they can summon when they need it."[2]

"It's strong and it flies. It flies the way Michael Jordan flies. It can make them fly."[3]

Connections

- **Childtimes**
- **Grown-ups Always Ask**

FOR YOUR READER'S LOG

What makes the relationship between brothers and sisters different than any other relationship? As you read "Childtimes" and "Grown-ups Always Ask," look for characteristics of sibling relationships. Write about these characteristics in your Reader's Log.

Odyssey Tours Child Travel Expert Advises Kids:

Traveling with adults is not always easy; they tend to get tired and cranky and often lose their tempers. To minimize this unpleasantness, follow this advice.

- Let adults sleep. If an adult falls asleep, do not ask "Are we there yet?" and poke at him or her. Adults will be in much better moods if they have had sufficient rest. This, of course, does not apply to an adult who is driving. This one should stay awake no matter how grouchy he or she gets.

- Let adults have their own music. This is important to them. Don't assume that they will want to lis-ten to the same music you do. If you have headphones for your own cassette player or portable CD player (or Ultra-Glide record player), so much the better.

- Let adults sit by the windows sometimes. Point out interesting sights as you travel. Ask them questions to keep them involved. For example, "Why are trees taller than grass?" and "Why do cows have four legs?" and

"When will it be dark?" and "Are we there yet?"

---

[1] From *Horn Book,* December 1975.

[2] From "Summon the Spirit" by Cassandra Spratling from *Detroit Free Press,* Online, World Wide Web; February 12, 1997.

[3] From "Summon the Spirit."

Novel Notes

The Watsons Go to Birmingham—1963 Connections

✶ NOVEL NOTES PROFILES ✶

Bernice Johnson Reagon

Notable work: Singer and founder of singing group Sweet Honey in the Rock; conceptual producer and host of the radio series *Wade in the Water: African American Sacred Music Traditions;* historian with Smithsonian Institution for 20 years; author of several books about music

Connections: Member of the Freedom Singers during the height of the civil rights movement

Present position: Professor of history at American University in Washington, D.C.

Walter Edward Fauntroy

Notable Achievements: Appointed by Dr. Martin Luther King, Jr., as Washington Bureau director of the Southern Christian Leadership Conference in 1960; served as District of Columbia coordinator of the March on Washington for Jobs and Freedom in 1963 and coordinator of the 1965 march from Selma to Montgomery, Alabama

Politics: Elected to House of Representatives as a Democrat in 1971

Connections

- **Two Interviews**
- **Schoolgirls Killed in Bombing**
- **Birmingham Sunday**
- **Alabama Burning**

FOR YOUR READER'S LOG

What gives people the courage and determination to participate in civil rights marches and demonstrations? You'll find some answers in these Connections pieces. Write notes in your Reader's Log as you read.

ASK the Professor

Dear Dr. I. Knoweverything,

A book I am reading talks about "freedom songs," and I don't get it. How can singing songs make anyone free?

　　　　　　　　—R. Zimmerman

Dear Mr. Zimmerman,

Some people agree with you that singing songs can't make anyone free. Julius Lester has said, "the days of singing freedom songs and the days of combating bullets and billy clubs with love are over." But freedom songs were an important part of the civil rights movement. Protesters sang them to remind themselves of their common purpose. Try to find a recording of "We Shall Overcome." Here are two verses:

WE SHALL OVERCOME

We shall overcome,
We shall overcome,
We shall overcome someday.
Oh, deep in my heart
I do believe,
We shall overcome someday.

We'll walk hand in hand,
We'll walk hand in hand,
We'll walk hand in hand someday.
Oh, deep in my heart
I do believe,
We shall overcome someday.

Lyrics from "We Shall Overcome," new words and arrangement by Zilphia Horton, Frank Hamilton, Guy Carawan, and Peter Seeger. Inspired by African American Gospel Singing, member of the Food & Tobacco Workers Union, Charleston SC, and the southern Civil Rights Movement. TRO - Copyright © 1960, 1963, and renewed © 1988, 1991 by **Ludlow Music Inc., New York.** International copyright secured. Reprinted by permission of the publisher.

Name _____

Reading Skills and Strategies Worksheet

Novel Organizer — *The Watsons Go to Birmingham—1963*

CHARACTER

Use the chart below to keep track of the characters in this book. Each time you come across a new character, write the character's name and the number of the page on which the character first appears. Then, jot down a brief description. Add information about the characters as you read. Put a star next to the name of each main character.

NAME OF CHARACTER	PAGE	DESCRIPTION

Reading Skills and Strategies Worksheet

Novel Organizer *(cont.)* *The Watsons Go to Birmingham—1963*

SETTING

Where and when does this story take place? ....

....

....

CONFLICT (Read at least one chapter before you answer.)

What is the biggest problem faced by the main character(s)? ....

....

....

How do you predict it will be resolved? ....

....

....

MAJOR EVENTS

- ....
- ....
- ....
- ....
-

OUTCOME

How is the main problem resolved? (How accurate was your prediction?) ....

....

....

Reading Skills and Strategies Worksheet

The Watsons Go to Birmingham—1963

Chapters 1–3: Contrasting Characters

Kenny and Byron may be brothers, but they are different in many ways. You have just met them, but you probably have learned enough about them to tell them apart easily. (Hint: Consider how they think, how they talk, how they treat others, and how they treat each other.)

In the separate ovals of this Venn diagram, write details from Chapters 1–3 that show how the brothers differ. Where the ovals overlap, note some ways in which the two Watsons are alike.

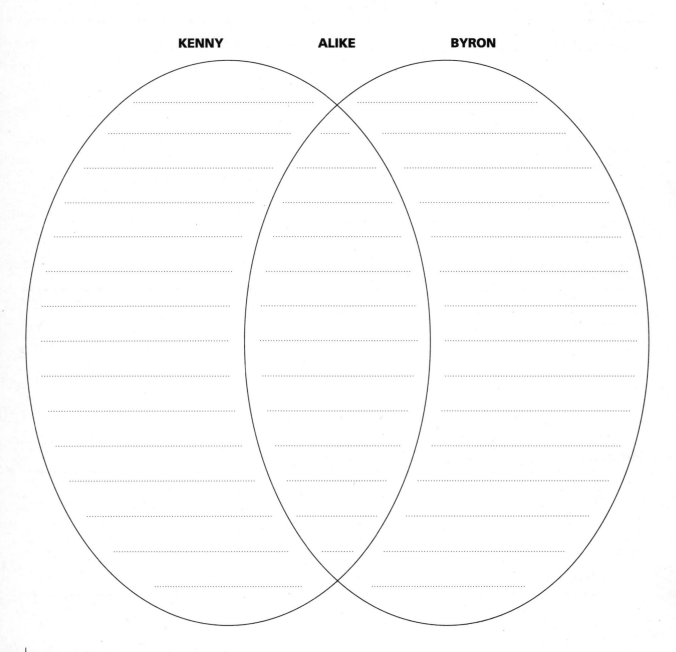

KENNY   ALIKE   BYRON

Reading Skills and Strategies Worksheet

The Watsons Go to Birmingham—1963

Chapters 4–7: Charting Causes and Effects

A **cause** is what makes something happen. The **effect** is what happens. Recognizing causes and effects can help you better understand what the events in a novel mean. For example, Kenny wanted a "personal saver" (cause), so he was glad to see two new students get on his school bus (effect).

Complete the following cause-and-effect chart. It will help you think about what happens in this part of the Watsons' story, and why.

CAUSE	EFFECT
Byron wants Joey to stop whining about wearing heavy winter clothes.	
	Byron makes Larry Dunn "star" in *The Great Carp Escape*.
Momma wants to teach Byron a lesson about the danger of fire.	
Byron learns that he can sign for food at Mitchell's.	
	Byron throws up the cookies and apples that he has eaten.
Against his parents' wishes, Byron gets a conk.	

Reading Skills and Strategies Worksheet

The Watsons Go to Birmingham—1963

Chapters 8–11: Responding to Quotations

Use the following chart to think about this part of the Watsons' story. **In the left-hand column, write interesting quotations from Chapters 8–11.** These might be about **characters, plot** details, **themes**—anything that catches your attention. **In the right-hand column, jot down a response to each quotation.** You might ask a question about it, describe how it makes you feel, or connect it to other stories that you have read.

QUOTATION	RESPONSE

Name _____ Date _____

Reading Skills and Strategies Worksheet

The Watsons Go to Birmingham—1963

Chapter 12–Epilogue: Exploring Character

One way to keep track of what happens during a novel is to focus on one character. Kenny goes through many major changes during the last four chapters of *The Watsons Go to Birmingham—1963*.

Explore what is happening to Kenny by completing this worksheet about specific events in these chapters.

1. *Chapter 12 event:* Kenny meets Mr. Robert.

   What Kenny says and does: ....

   What Kenny is thinking and feeling: ....

   ....

2. *Chapter 13 event:* At Collier's Landing, Kenny meets the Wool Pooh.

   What Kenny says and does: ....

   What Kenny is thinking and feeling: ....

   ....

3. *Chapter 14 event:* Kenny looks inside the church.

   What Kenny says and does: ....

   What Kenny is thinking and feeling: ....

   ....

4. *Chapter 15 event:* Kenny stays in the World-Famous Watson Pet Hospital.

   What Kenny says and does: ....

   What Kenny is thinking and feeling: ....

   ....

5. *Chapter 15 event:* Kenny talks to Byron in the bathroom.

   What Kenny says and does: ....

   What Kenny is thinking and feeling: ....

   ....

Literary Elements Worksheet
The Watsons Go to Birmingham—1963

Allusion

An **allusion** is a reference to someone or something from literature, history, religion, mythology, or another field. Many of the allusions in *The Watsons Go to Birmingham—1963* come from "popular culture," such as movies, songs, and television programs.

Explain the following allusions. (The first one is done for you. Sometimes more than one meaning is possible.)

_____

1. *Allusion:* When Kenny and Joey wear their winter clothes, kids at school say, "Here come some of them Weird Watsons doing their Mummy imitations."

   This allusion suggests that being bundled up in heavy clothes makes them walk stiffly, with their arms out. The movie monster called the Mummy walks in the same way.

2. *Allusion:* As Momma plays with Byron's conked hair, she calls him "Bozo," after the television clown.

   This allusion suggests that ....

   ....

   ....

3. *Allusion:* Grandma Sands laughs "just like the Wicked Witch of the West," the villain of the movie *The Wizard of Oz.*

   This allusion suggests that ....

   ....

   ....

4. *Allusion:* When Byron meets Grandma Sands, "it was like Dracula [the vampire] and a giraffe, and Byron was all neck."

   This allusion suggests that ....

   ....

   ....

5. *Allusion:* Toward the end of the novel, Byron brings Kenny along when he goes to play basketball. Kenny comments that "you didn't have to be Albert Einstein [the brilliant scientist] to figure out" that Byron threatened the big guys into letting Kenny play.

   This allusion suggests that ....

   ....

Name _____ Date _____

Literary Elements Worksheet

The Watsons Go to Birmingham—1963

Atmosphere / Mood

The Watsons Go to Birmingham—1963 has a well-developed **atmosphere** or **mood**—that is, a clear sense of the "feeling" of the story. The atmosphere changes during the novel—in some cases, from chapter to chapter.

Briefly describe the overall atmosphere of each chapter listed below. Then, give examples of details that help create that atmosphere.

CHAPTER	ATMOSPHERE	DETAILS
1		
5		
13		
15		

Name _____ Date _____

Literary Elements Worksheet

The Watsons Go to Birmingham—1963

Conflict

As the Watsons' story unfolds, various characters face **conflicts.** Some are
external conflicts, or struggles with outside forces. Others are **internal
conflicts,** which take place within a character's mind.

**On the following chart, describe three of the external conflicts in
the novel and two of the internal conflicts. Explain how each conflict
is resolved.**

EXTERNAL CONFLICT	RESOLUTION
1.	
2.	
3.	

INTERNAL CONFLICT	RESOLUTION
1.	
2.	

Glossary

The Watsons Go to Birmingham—1963

- Words are listed by chapter in order of appearance.
- The definition and part of speech are based on the way the word is used in the chapter. For other uses of the word, check a dictionary.
- **Vocabulary Words** are preceded by an asterisk (*) and appear in the Vocabulary Worksheets.

Chapter 1

thermostat *n.:* device for controlling temperature

juvenile delinquent *n.:* person under 18 who gets into a lot of trouble

landlord *n.:* person who rents property to others

flypaper *n.:* sticky paper made to catch flies

Chapter 2

*****hostile** *adj.:* unfriendly; threatening

*****incapable** *adj.:* not able

*****assure** *v.:* encourage by promising

*****intimidate** *v.:* to bully or threaten

*****emulate** *v.:* imitate; copy

*****bravo** *interj.:* very good

*****punctual** *adj.:* on time

Chapter 3

*****desperate** *adj.:* wanting intensely

reinforcements *n.:* additional or supporting forces

radioactive *adj.:* giving off dangerous levels of nuclear radiation

pliers *n.:* a tool used for gripping or bending objects

Chapter 4

zombie *n.:* person in a sleeplike state and with a strange appearance

*****hypnotized** *adj.:* in a trance-like state

frostbite *n.:* freezing or partial freezing of part of the body

Chapter 5

flamethrower *n.:* a weapon that shoots fire

traitor *adj.:* betraying

Chapter 6

peon *n.:* impoverished laborer, especially one who does menial work

conscience *n.:* sense of right and wrong

Chapter 7

linoleum *n.:* smooth floor tiles

*****tolerate** *v.:* put up with

Chapter 8

ultimate *n.:* something that is the greatest or highest possible

*****pinnacle** *n.:* peak; highest point

seniority *n.:* privilege that comes from being older

*****dispersal** *n.:* condition of being spread out or scattered

phonic *adj.:* having to do with sound

*****exclusive** *adj.:* unique

*****grasped** *v.:* understood; realized

*****haphazardly** *adv.:* randomly; by chance

*****hacked** *v.:* carelessly cut; chopped

technician *n.:* person who is expert in the mechanics of some device or machine

*****enhance** *v.:* improve; make better

*****patter** *n.:* informal, rapid chatter

*****swoon** *v.:* faint

*****maestro** *n.:* master of an art, such as a musical conductor

The Watsons Go to Birmingham—1963

Chapter 9

accustomed *v.:* get used to something

***eavesdropped** *v.:* listened secretly

***grapevine** *n.:* an informal means of spreading information from person to person

transferred *v.:* moved; sent

***offended** *v.:* had one's feelings hurt; was insulted

Chapter 10

sanitation *adj.:* relating to hygiene, especially a clean water supply

***facilities** *n.:* rooms or buildings used for a special purpose, such as restrooms and restaurants

Chapter 11

pathetic *adj.:* inspiring pity

bad-dispositioned *adj.:* unhappy and irritable

***frequencies** *n.:* the tone or level of sound vibrations

Chapter 12

wilier *adj.:* more crafty or sly

***scolding** *v.:* correcting angrily; nagging

Chapter 13

***whirlpool** *n.:* dangerously spinning body of water

***electrocuted** *v.:* killed with an electrical shock

Chapter 14

sonic boom *n.:* an explosive sound caused by planes moving faster than the speed of sound

***fluttered** *v.:* shook rapidly; trembled

Chapter 15

curveballs *n.:* baseball pitches that unexpectedly change direction

Epilogue

***amended** *v.:* changed; revised

discrimination *n.:* show of prejudice or bias against a group of people or an individual in that group

***pervasive** *adj.:* widespread

prohibited *v.:* outlawed; forbidden

interracial *adj.:* between people of different races

***segregation** *n.:* practice of keeping different races or groups of people apart

***strove** *v.:* tried hard

***sit-ins** *n.:* protests in which people sit down in a place and refuse to leave

boycotts *n.:* protests in which people refuse to buy someone's merchandise or use someone's services

banned *v.:* made illegal; forbade

picketing *n.:* marching or standing outside a business, government building, or other place and carrying signs to show opposition to a policy or practice

***demonstrations** *n.:* public meetings or parades in which people show how they feel about an issue

***confrontations** *n.:* acts of opposing or standing face to face against someone or something

Vocabulary Worksheet 1   Chapters 1–8

The Watsons Go to Birmingham—1963

A. Match each word in the left-hand column with the correct meaning from the right-hand column. Write the letter of the definition in the space provided.

_____	**1.** intimidate	**a.**	spreading out
_____	**2.** hypnotized	**b.**	unique
_____	**3.** maestro	**c.**	chopped
_____	**4.** emulate	**d.**	very good
_____	**5.** bravo	**e.**	master of an art
_____	**6.** swoon	**f.**	wanting intensely
_____	**7.** hacked	**g.**	threaten
_____	**8.** dispersal	**h.**	copy
_____	**9.** exclusive	**i.**	faint
_____	**10.** desperate	**j.**	in a trancelike state

B. *Antonyms* are words that have the opposite, or nearly the opposite, meaning. Choose the antonym for the word in bold type. Write the letter of that antonym in the space provided.

_____ **11. hostile: (a)** angry **(b)** friendly **(c)** funny **(d)** useful

_____ **12. haphazardly: (a)** rarely **(b)** casually **(c)** neatly **(d)** safely

_____ **13. pinnacle: (a)** summit **(b)** depth **(c)** confusion **(d)** problem

_____ **14. incapable: (a)** skilled **(b)** guilty **(c)** foolish **(d)** healthy

_____ **15. patter: (a)** secret **(b)** rattle **(c)** silence **(d)** conversation

_____ **16. punctual: (a)** timely **(b)** violent **(c)** late **(d)** frequent

_____ **17. tolerate: (a)** oppose **(b)** accept **(c)** adore **(d)** prefer

_____ **18. enhance: (a)** build **(b)** deny **(c)** improve **(d)** damage

_____ **19. assure: (a)** scold **(b)** pledge **(c)** hint **(d)** discourage

_____ **20. grasped: (a)** was confused by **(b)** understood **(c)** held tightly **(d)** chose

Vocabulary Worksheet 2   Chapter 9–Epilogue

The Watsons Go to Birmingham—1963

A. Write the word from the box that best completes each sentence on
the line provided. (You will not use every word.)

pervasive	fluttered	facilities	offended
segregation	strove	confrontations	scolding
sit-ins	grapevine	demonstrations	amended

1. My elderly neighbor began working for civil rights when, as a young man, he was
   _____ at the way African Americans were treated.

2. He was there when African Americans staged _____ at lunch counters,
   refusing to move until they were served.

3. He took part in many _____, including the one that 200,000 civil rights
   activists attended in Washington, D.C.

4. Discrimination was _____, affecting African Americans throughout
   the country.

5. He recalls a time when restrooms and other public _____ were separate
   for blacks and whites.

6. Often, he would hear through the _____ that someone failed to get a
   job because he or she was African American.

7. Fortunately, many people have _____ their views, and greater racial
   harmony exists.

8. Children of all races attend the same schools; _____ is not legal.

9. Fewer racial _____ occur today than when my neighbor began his efforts.

10. He _____ to end discrimination and has been pleased to see the progress
    that has been made.

B. In an *analogy,* pairs of words are related in the same way.
Use words from the box below to complete the following analogies.

11. tornado : wind :: _____ : water

12. bumped : crashed :: shocked : _____

13. heard : _____ :: saw : spied

electrocuted
frequencies
whirlpool
eavesdropped

Name _____ Date _____

TEST PART I: OBJECTIVE QUESTIONS

In the space provided, mark each true statement *T* and each false statement *F*. (20 points)

_____ **1.** Kenny's lips freeze to the car mirror when he kisses it.

_____ **2.** Kenny shares his gloves with Rufus.

_____ **3.** Larry Dunn bullies Byron.

_____ **4.** Joey saves Byron from getting his fingers burned.

_____ **5.** Byron kills a mourning dove by throwing a cookie at it.

_____ **6.** The Ultra-Glide is Dad's car, which everyone calls the Brown Bomber.

_____ **7.** Joey is excited about the angel she receives as a gift.

_____ **8.** Byron talks Kenny into going swimming at Collier's Landing.

_____ **9.** Byron says that the Wool Pooh is Winnie-the-Pooh's evil twin.

_____ **10.** Kenny spends time behind the couch after the family returns from Alabama.

Complete each statement by writing the letter of the best answer in the space provided. (10 points)

11. The kids at school make fun of Kenny because _____.

    a. his father is unemployed   **c.** he has a strong Southern accent
    b. he has a lazy eye and is smart   **d.** he plays with toy dinosaurs

12. When Byron gets a conk, _____.

    a. Joey protects him   **c.** Momma tries to burn his fingers
    b. Dad shaves Byron's head   **d.** he won't let Kenny play "Yakety Yak"

13. The Watsons travel to Birmingham because _____.

    a. Momma and Dad want Byron to   **c.** Kenny is depressed over what
        stay with Grandma Sands   he has seen at the church
    b. Grandma Sands has never seen   **d.** Momma wants to meet Mr. Robert
        any of her grandchildren

14. When Kenny goes to Collier's Landing, he _____.

    a. hears an explosion and runs home   **c.** saves Byron from drowning
    b. stays out of the water   **d.** sees Joey as an angel

15. After the bomb explodes, Kenny _____.

    a. rushes into the church and saves Joey   **c.** looks into the church and sees
                             the Wool Pooh
    b. stays home with Grandma Sands   **d.** watches from a distance

TEST   PART II: SHORT-ANSWER QUESTIONS

Answer each question, using the lines provided. *(40 points)*

16. Kenny plays with LJ even though LJ keeps stealing his dinosaurs. What does this tell you about Kenny?

....

....

....

17. What happens after Kenny hurts Rufus's feelings by laughing at Larry Dunn's joke?

....

....

....

18. How does Byron react when he learns that Larry Dunn has stolen Kenny's gloves?

....

....

....

19. Explain why Momma reacts as she does when she catches Byron playing with matches.

....

....

....

20. Why does Byron get sick after he and Kenny eat the Swedish Cremes?

....

....

....

Name _____ Date _____

 **PART II: SHORT-ANSWER QUESTIONS** *(continued)*

Answer each question, using the lines provided.

21. What makes Momma and Dad so angry when Byron gets a conk?

....

....

....

22. Why is Momma upset with Dad when he decides to drive straight through to Birmingham? (Give two reasons.)

....

....

....

23. Why does Byron go to Collier's Landing?

....

....

....

24. At the church, whom does Joey see and follow to safety? Why is that detail important?

....

....

....

25. What is the purpose of the Epilogue to this novel?

....

....

....

TEST PART III: ESSAY QUESTIONS

Choose *two* of the following topics. Use your own paper to write two or three paragraphs about each topic you choose. (*30 points*)

a. The **setting** is the time and the place in which a story takes place. Describe the setting of *The Watsons Go to Birmingham—1963*. Then, explain its importance to this novel. Support your explanation with details from the novel.

b. This novel begins with a series of very humorous episodes. Then the Watsons go to Birmingham, and the story turns frightening and sad. What **mood** or "feeling" does Christopher Paul Curtis leave you with when the novel ends? Is it humorous, serious, optimistic or pessimistic? Give details from the novel to support your answer.

c. Byron is a "juvenile delinquent" in Flint, but he changes his ways as soon as the Watsons reach Birmingham. Kenny is an obedient, quiet boy in Flint, but his behavior begins to change as soon as he reaches Grandma Sands's door. How would you explain the changes in these two **characters**?

d. A **theme** is a main idea in a work of literature. It's a message that the author wants to convey. There may be several themes in a novel. What do you think is the main theme of *The Watsons Go to Birmingham—1963*? Support your opinion with details from different parts of the novel.

e. Many good stories teach as well as entertain. How did reading *The Watsons Go to Birmingham—1963* help you understand the world at that time? How did it help you understand people and life today?

___

Use this space to make notes.

Answer Key

Chapters 1–3: Making Meanings

> **READING CHECK**
> Students in each group should take turns retelling each of the major adventures described in Chapters 1–3: Byron's getting stuck to the mirror; Kenny's reading to the fifth-grade class; Kenny and Rufus's growing friendship; Kenny's loss of dinosaurs to LJ.

1. Answers will vary. Both Kenny and Rufus have more than their fair share of fun poked at them. Many students will say that Rufus has the harder time because he is a new student whose accent and clothes make him stand out. He doesn't have Byron to help him out occasionally, as Kenny does.

2. Byron is cool, tough, strong, stubborn, lazy, and narcissistic. His actions seem motivated by pride or the desire to appear cool to others.

3. Dad probably knows that it is not a serious problem; he also recognizes the humor of it. He probably also knows that Byron enjoys giving Kenny and other kids a hard time, and he may think that being on the receiving end of the joke may teach Byron a lesson.

4. Answers will vary. The novel begins with Kenny's description of the temperature as "about a zillion degrees below zero"—his way of emphasizing the cold. When Byron's lips freeze to the car mirror, Kenny ponders the seriousness of the situation and wonders if the family would "be driving around in the summer with a skeleton dangling from the outside mirror by its lips." Comparing the tough kids at school, Kenny says that "Larry [Dunn] was the king of Clark . . . but Byron was a god."

5. The episode shows that Kenny really is a child, not an adult "voice" pretending to be a child. The way he allows himself to be fooled during the game helps to show his innocence and immaturity; it also helps to show how much he needs a true friend like Rufus.

6. Some students may feel that Rufus is not a "personal saver" because no one could match Kenny's idealization of such a character. Many students, however, may feel that Rufus fills the bill because his friendship "saves" Kenny from the need to be with kids who take advantage of him.

7. Many students would not like the experience because they want to fit in and be like the other students. Being put on display makes them stand out and feel "different." Some students might feel comfortable enough with themselves not to mind.

8. Kenny probably would have stood up for Rufus and made the other students leave him alone.

9. Most students will agree the dialogue is realistic. It includes informal and nonstandard English that many people use in everyday speech. The dialogue includes slang, such as *cool* and *punk*. The children use double negatives and words such as *ain't, gotta,* and *'bout*. They drop linking verbs, as in *we gotta see if you ready to graduate* and *you done so good*.

Chapters 4–7: Making Meanings

> **READING CHECK**
> Students should create illustrations for the main episodes in this section. These could include frozen people, the stolen gloves, playing with matches, the Swedish Cremes, and the conk.

1. Students may or may not like Byron, but they should recognize that he is not all bad, for he occasionally does help out his brother and sister.

2. Kenny is more sensitive than the others, perhaps because he has been bullied so much himself. He doesn't like violence.

3. Byron is embarrassed to think that his family might receive welfare food, or that they aren't capable of paying for food. Momma is more practical and tells Byron that while they're not on welfare, they have been before and would be again if they had to.

4. They are displeased with his disobedience; they especially do not like the fact that he is unhappy with his real African American hair. They also do not consider him old enough to be making that kind of decision without asking them about it.

5. Answers will vary, but many students will name the revelation of Byron's conk—and the results of it. Students should identify a scene from these chapters and explain what they thought was humorous about it.

6. Students may conclude that Joey is the most mature. She does not participate in adventures like the ones that get Byron in trouble. She takes responsibility for helping her brothers; but unlike Byron when he bullies Larry Dunn, she doesn't look for a way to get personal enjoyment out of it. She counsels Byron about how to avoid getting in trouble. Unlike Kenny, she does not enjoy Byron's embarrassment when he gets his head shaved.

7. Opinions will vary. Students may consider this punishment extreme, while others may feel that it was the only way to impress upon Byron the dangers of fire.

8. Responses will vary widely, but students should explain why the techniques they have suggested would work for Byron in particular, based on what they know about his personality.

9. Many student's will not consider Joey's actions unusual, citing instances when they or others have risked punishment to protect someone else. Others might think that a kindergartner would be too afraid to take the action that Joey did. Either way, responses should be supported with examples.

Chapters 8–11: Making Meanings

> **READING CHECK**
>
> **a.** It is a record player for a car.
>
> **b.** Momma is both organized and cautious; she is aware that, in 1963, black families traveling through the South cannot stop just anywhere they please. In many places, they are not welcome, and stopping is not safe.
>
> **c.** Dad decides to drive straight through to Alabama instead of stopping. As a result, much of Momma's work in planning the trip is wasted.
>
> **d.** She is small and thin—not the physically intimidating person that he expected.

1. Answers will vary. Some students may feel that the trip was rather boring, since everyone except Dad slept quite a bit. Parts of the trip, such as the outhouses, were unpleasant. Still, the night sky from the mountaintop and the ride through the dark with their hands out the window were fun and memorable for the family.

2. The dialogue is funny but loving at the same time. It helps fill out the characterization of Dad and underscores the theme that families can be a great source of strength and encouragement.

3. Dad's reasons include wanting Byron to see how difficult life will be in the face of discrimination and removing him from the temptations that have gotten him into increasing trouble in Flint.

4. Students may suggest that Byron was just bragging to Buphead and that he had no intention of staying silent. Others may say that Byron forgot about his plan in the excitement of the trip.

5. The scene itself is rather scary, and the stop was not a part of Momma's plan. Furthermore, this was in the South in the 1960s, where terrible things sometimes happened to African Americans. It would be easy to become frightened in that setting.

6. Kenny sees Grandma as Dracula, the vampire, and Byron as a giraffe, with plenty of neck for her to bite. He means that the big confrontation between Grandma and Byron isn't going to materialize.

7. Answers will vary. Students should provide an example and explain how this person met their expectations or surprised them.

8. Responses will vary. Some of the qualities students might list include authority, dignity, fairness, confidence, and respect for themselves and others.

9. Some students may conclude that the story contributes to the development of the character of Joey. Others may sense its importance as foreshadowing or as a symbol which will be explained later.

Chapter 12–Epilogue: **Making Meanings**

> **READING CHECK**
>
> a. Kenny goes swimming and is caught in a whirlpool, which he thinks is the Wool Pooh trying to drown him. Byron saves Kenny.
>
> b. The Wool Pooh is Winnie-the-Pooh's evil twin brother.
>
> c. A bomb explodes, destroying the church and killing four little girls. Joey leaves the church just before the explosion.
>
> d. Kenny can't get over his experiences at the church in Birmingham. He feels scared and embarrassed by what he saw and how he acted. Byron helps him get over his shame and fear.

1. Answers will vary. Many students will remember thinking that Kenny was getting himself into trouble by going to the lake, that the family was lucky when Joey came home safe, and that Byron turned out to be a good brother when he helped Kenny out of his depression.

2. Students may conclude that Byron is beginning to become more responsible and mature. Kenny,

however, is reaching an age where he wants to explore, have adventures, and rebel. Their personalities are changing.

3. Students should recognize that there is an ironic contrast between the freedom and rights represented by "the red, white, and blue" and the attempt to stifle freedom and rights represented by the bombing.

4. Answers will vary. Some students may suggest that it was a stranger who looked like Kenny. Others may say it was an angel or some "part" of Kenny (as Byron later suggests).

5. Students should see that Byron indeed has changed. He has learned more about the value of family and has concluded that it is all right to care about someone and to show it. He also may be realizing that he can be a big influence in helping Kenny.

6. Most students will say that it supports Kenny's view. Even Byron cannot provide a natural explanation for Joey's escape from the bombing. Furthermore, Kenny's talk about the magic of family love and understanding represents one of the major themes of the novel.

7. Answers will be personal and need not be shared. Most students will acknowledge that the power of suggestion is strong and can encourage people to experience things that do not exist.

8. Most students should be aware that hate crimes remain a part of American society. Racist actions may not be as overt and common as they once were, but they still occur.

9. Students who would have moved the Epilogue to the beginning of the book might consider it an effective way to set the stage for the novel's climax—and give readers a hint of where the story is leading. Students who would have kept it at the end may prefer to retain the element of surprise, so that neither the readers nor the characters would expect the bombing.

Answer Key (continued)   *The Watsons Go to Birmingham—1963*

Exploring the Connections

Childtimes: Making Meanings

> **READING CHECK**
> **a.** She describes the "white city," occupied by the president and all the white people, and the "black city," where she lives.
>
> **b.** Examples include separate swimming pools, African Americans not being allowed to sit at the soda fountains, whites being served first in stores, "White Only" jobs, segregated housing, and white newspapers not carrying news affecting African Americans.
>
> **c.** They go to visit relatives.

1. Some students may prefer the city with its many vendors and things to do. Others may prefer Parmele because it is a quiet town, has farm animals, and introduces many of the author's relatives. They also may prefer it because there is no mention of the racism that seems so prevalent in Washington, D.C.

2. The vendors help establish the setting as the early part of the twentieth century. They also provide a sense of the activity and bustle of the city.

3. Greenfield acknowledges both good and bad things about the city, but her tone is basically one of fond recollection.

4. The two trips are similar. Both are made in old cars; in both, the children play games and argue. Both are journeys from the North to the South, and both families are aware of the racism around them. The Watsons have a brush with violence in the South, however, whereas Greenfield's family enjoys a safe visit to Parmele.

5. Answers will vary. Students should understand that they can read nonfiction for both information and enjoyment. They may respond strongly to the accounts of segregation, knowing that Greenfield is telling about actual conditions. The family relationships may be appealing because they are real, as well.

Grown-ups Always Ask: Making Meanings

> **READING CHECK**
> It is important to remember that the fight won't last forever and that there are more important things than fighting.

1. Answers will be personal and need not be shared. Even students who have no brothers or sisters should recognize the realism in the poem.

2. "Any reason" is an excuse for fighting brought about when one sibling annoys another—for example, by name-calling or hogging the bathroom. "No reason" is a result of one child's having a bad day that may have nothing to do with the brother or sister.

3. The poem suggests that siblings are the only people you can count on—and you can count on them completely.

4. The relationships are very similar. In each, brothers and sisters fight and tease and make life miserable for each other. In each, however, the brothers and sisters stick together to help, protect, and support each other.

5. Students may conclude that the speaker is simply explaining that fighting happens, and that it is a part of the normal sibling relationship. The speaker is saying that even if you do fight with your brothers and sisters, trusting and relying upon the other sibling is far more important.

Two Interviews: Making Meanings

> **READING CHECK**
> **a.** She sang.
> **b.** Connor directed his police officers to use billy clubs and fire hoses to attack and arrest the protesters, even in front of television cameras.

1. Most students will admire the actions taken by Reagon and Fauntroy, recognizing that it took

great courage and faith in their beliefs to act, in spite of their fears about the violence and hatred directed at them.

2. He means that the violence and brutality toward African Americans in Birmingham, which was filmed and broadcast to people throughout the country, made all Americans aware of and concerned about the injustices suffered by African Americans.

3. He quotes from the Bible to justify his involvement. He sees the ministry and civil rights activism as different ways of setting people free.

4. Students should recognize that the atmosphere and setting of the novel arise from the actual conditions and events that Reagon and Fauntroy discuss.

5. Many students will say that music gives them courage, makes them happy, makes them feel better when they are sad, or helps them feel more sociable when they're with others.

Schoolgirls Killed in Bombing
Making Meanings

READING CHECK
People were gathering for a special children's church service. The four girls were in the ladies lounge in the basement of the church, preparing for their parts in the service. The bomb had already been placed under a staircase outside the church.

1. Many students may express sadness at the deaths, anger at the needless violence, shock that someone would bomb a church and kill children, or surprise at the open racism of the police commissioner.

2. Students will probably say that King was correct. The tragedy made many whites aware of the consequences of racial hatred. A white Southern lawyer acknowledged that all people who allowed the hatred to spread contributed to the

violence. The bombing also brought the civil rights issue to national attention. It brought about fresh support for federal civil rights legislation.

3. Answers will vary. Students may feel that the case was not pursued because the victims were black, the perpetrators were white, and racism was rampant.

4. In the novel, Kenny personally witnesses the destruction from a bombing based on this event. By reading the facts, the reader gets a sense of the violence of the event and the suffering of real people. The reader then can better imagine what Kenny witnessed and why it would affect him so strongly.

Birmingham Sunday: **Making Meanings**

READING CHECK
a. They are the four little girls who died in the bombing of the church.
b. It is the basement wall that was spattered with the blood of the little girls who were killed in the bombing.

1. Students may find some of the references hard to understand, but many students will appreciate the poem because it expresses deeply felt emotions and the speaker's hopes, which may correspond to their own feelings.

2. The repetition emphasizes that the bombing took innocent lives.

3. Possible answers include equality, justice, and freedom—ideals that, at the time, were only beginning to become a reality for African Americans.

4. Students may feel that the poem is a more intellectual and analytical response to the tragedy. The speaker did not witness the event but speaks about it as an interested observer. Kenny's emotions were real and intense, as

might be expected from someone who had witnessed the scene personally.

5. Some students may say that today there is greater equality, less discrimination, and less violence and racism than in 1963. Other students may argue that many of these same problems still exist and that the songs that will awaken the girls have not yet been sung.

Alabama Burning: **Making Meanings**

> **READING CHECK**
>
> **a.** It is a political documentary about the bombing of the Sixteenth Street Baptist Church. It includes historical footage as well as interviews with relatives and friends of the victims and with civil rights activists who were in Birmingham that year.
>
> **b.** McNair wanted the story to be told so that people would know what really happened. He trusted Lee to do it properly and accurately.

1. Many students will say that the article makes them want to see the film because it emphasizes the care with which the film was made. The historical footage and the interviews with people connected to the victims and to the event will appeal to many students.

2. Students may suggest that as an African American, McNair had long experience with people taking advantage of him. As the father of one of the victims of the bombing, he doubtless talked with many people—police and FBI as well as reporters. He probably learned from talking to them, observing their actions, and hearing what they said, that many were not interested in the truth.

3. Most students will agree that this story is important. Perhaps it will make more people aware of the causes of the tragedy and thereby prevent hate crimes from happening in the future.

4. Students may suggest that although the novel is fictional, it offers insights into the historical period and the attitudes and feelings of people who confronted such violent, unpredictable, and senseless racism.

5. Some students will agree with McNair that later bombers might have committed crimes thinking that they would go unpunished, having seen the weak pusuit of justice in Birmingham. Others may note that violence seems to breed more violence, whether it is punished or not— the earlier crime may have inspired the later one. Other students may feel that the bombings were unconnected except as random acts of violence, perhaps both inspired by the climate of hate McNair notes.

Reading Skills and Strategies Worksheets

Chapters 1–3: **Contrasting Characters**

See the following diagram for some possible answers.

KENNY	ALIKE	BYRON
close to Joey; wanting to be closer to Byron	brothers	independent and "tough"
obedient	students at Clark Elementary	rebellious
good student	supportive of each other when trouble arises	skips school often

Chapters 4–7: Charting Causes and Effects

See the following for a suggested chart.

CAUSE	EFFECT
Byron wants Joey to stop whining about wearing heavy winter clothes.	He tells her a story about the "fake garbage trucks" that pick up people who have frozen solid.
Larry steals Kenny's gloves.	Byron makes Larry Dunn "star" in *The Great Carp Escape*.
Momma wants to teach Byron a lesson about the danger of fire.	Momma tries to burn Byron's fingers with matches.
Byron learns that he can sign for food at Mitchell's.	He gets two bags of cookies by signing on the family's account at the store.
Byron hits and kills a mourning dove with a cookie.	Byron throws up the cookies and apples that he has eaten.
Against his parents' wishes, Byron gets a conk.	Dad shaves Byron's head.

Chapters 8–11: Responding to Quotations

Quotations will vary. One possible quotation with a suggested response for each of the four chapters follows.

QUOTATION	RESPONSE
"Well, I don't believe it! If you squint your eyes and look real hard, there's no doubt about it, this boy's got a real mustache going here!"	Dad seems tough at times, but he loves Kenny. He's encouraging his son without being too obvious about it.
"I guess you really showed them, didn't you? Boy, they were really begging you to talk, weren't they, Daddy-O?"	Way to go, Kenny! Byron talks big, but he still wants the attention. If I were Kenny, I would have said the same thing!
"[I]nstead of seeing the normal amount of stars it looked like there had been a star explosion. There were more stars in the sky than empty space."	I remember a time when I saw the sky looking like this. I wonder what "the normal amount of stars" means to Kenny?
"[A]s the Weird Watsons stood there with some of us laughing, some of us crying and some of us looking cool it felt like we all were wrapped up in a big ball."	That's a great word picture—it shows how people can be different but still belong together. That "wrapped up in a big ball" feeling is great, too!

Chapter 12–Epilogue
Exploring Character

1. *Chapter 12 event:* Kenny meets Mr. Robert.

   What Kenny says and does: listens to Mr. Robert's story about his coon dog and to Momma's questions to Grandma Sands about him; doesn't say much

   What Kenny is thinking and feeling: likes Mr. Robert but isn't sure about the relationship between him and Grandma Sands, especially when she scolds Momma for being upset about it; the scolding itself also interests him because he gets to see Momma in the "child" role

2. *Chapter 13 event:* At Collier's Landing, Kenny meets the Wool Pooh.

   What Kenny says and does: goes swimming but cannot escape the pull of the current; laughs at first and then cries for help

What Kenny is thinking and feeling: cockiness quickly turns to fear; begins to panic, thinking that he will die; sure that the Wool Pooh is a real creature; watches the Wool Pooh and Byron fighting over him.

3. *Chapter 14 event:* Kenny looks inside the church.

What Kenny says and does: says nothing but looks into the church; sees wreckage, upset people, and two little girls lying on the ground; pulls a shoe away from the Wool Pooh

What Kenny is thinking and feeling: confused about what has happened; worried about finding Joey; thinks that she has died in the explosion

4. *Chapter 15 event:* Kenny stays in the World-Famous Watson Pet Hospital.

What Kenny says and does: remains behind the couch, rarely coming out; listens to his parents talking about him; turns down Byron's invitations to come out

What Kenny is thinking and feeling: confused and sad about the things he saw after the bombing; worried that the violence will reach him at home

5. *Chapter 15 event:* Kenny talks to Byron in the bathroom.

What Kenny says and does: looks at himself in the mirror; cries for a long time, letting Byron hold him; listens to Byron's explanation about the bombing and his encouragement that Kenny will be all right

What Kenny is thinking and feeling: needs to put his thoughts in order; comes to a greater sense of himself and his ability to survive; realizes that his brother really does love him

Literary Elements Worksheets

Allusion

2. *This allusion suggests that* Byron's newly reddish, stiff hair looks ridiculous. It makes him look like a clown (and Bozo the clown had stiff red hair)—not cool, as he had hoped.

3. *This allusion suggests that* her laugh is like a cackle, and perhaps the Watson children wonder if she is evil, like the witch in *The Wizard of Oz*.

4. *This allusion suggests that* Grandma Sands is more than a match for Byron. Despite his clever toughness, Grandma will best him at every turn.

5. *This allusion suggests that* Byron's threat was very evident. Albert Einstein was a brilliant scientist, but a person didn't need to be brilliant to know that Byron forced his friends to include Kenny.

Atmosphere / Mood

See the following for a suggested chart.

Chapter	Atmosphere	Details
1	fun	exaggerated description of the cold and of other characters; Dad's jokes; Byron's freezing his lips to the car mirror
5	tense	references to fire; Momma's anger and "snake-woman voice"; Joey's and then Byron's tears; the attempted match-burnings
13	terrifying	the warning signs at Collier's Landing; the description of the Wool Pooh; Kenny's sudden realization that he has

		been caught; his failed attempts to get away; the battle between Byron and the Wool Pooh
15	serious but hopeful	the "magic" of the World-Famous Watson Pet Hospital; Kenny's greater friendship with Byron; Byron's holding Kenny when he cries and encouraging him

Conflict

See the following for a suggested chart.

EXTERNAL CONFLICT	RESOLUTION
1. Byron disobeys his parents repeatedly.	His parents take him to Alabama so that Grandma Sands can deal with him. Because of his experiences there, he seems to outgrow much of his rebelliousness.
2. Joey doesn't want Momma to break her promise to God, but she also doesn't want to see Byron get burned.	As Momma lights the matches, Joey blows them out.
3. Larry Dunn bullies Kenny and steals his gloves.	Byron steps in, getting Kenny's gloves back and teaching Larry a lesson about being a bully.

INTERNAL CONFLICT	RESOLUTION
1. Kenny had hoped that Rufus Fry would take his place as the target of the school's bullies, but he finds that Rufus expects to be friends with him.	The two set aside their differences and become good friends.

| 2. Kenny wrestles with the memories of the church bombing. | Byron encourages him and helps him put things into perspective. |

Vocabulary Worksheets

Vocabulary Worksheet 1

If you wish to score this worksheet, assign the point values given in parentheses.

A. *(5 points each)*   **B.** *(5 points each)*

1. g 6. i   11. b 16. c
2. j 7. c   12. c 17. a
3. e 8. a   13. b 18. d
4. h 9. b   14. a 19. d
5. d 10. f 15. c 20. a

Vocabulary Worksheet 2

If you wish to score this worksheet, assign the point values given in parentheses.

A. *(7 points each)*

1. offended 6. grapevine
2. sit-ins 7. amended
3. demonstrations 8. segregation
4. pervasive 9. confrontations
5. facilities 10. strove

B. *(10 points each)*

11. whirlpool 12. electrocuted
13. eavesdropped

Test

Part I: Objective Questions

1. F 6. F 11. b
2. T 7. F 12. b
3. F 8. F 13. a
4. T 9. T 14. d
5. T 10. T 15. c

Part II: Short-Answer Questions

16. Kenny doesn't have many friends, so he's willing to put up with LJ just to have a playmate.

17. Although Kenny could not help laughing, he immediately regrets it. Rufus stops talking to him, sharing Kenny's lunch, and playing with him despite Kenny's attempt to apologize. Only after Kenny's mother intervenes does Rufus decide to be friends with him again.

18. At first, Byron wants to help Kenny and punish Larry for stealing the gloves. Then he gets carried away with being mean in front of an audience, making Larry "star" in *The Great Carp Escape.*

19. Momma is angry at Byron and frightened that he will start a fire one day that will kill him and the other children. She wants to teach him a lesson about the seriousness of fire.

20. Byron is upset and sick to his stomach because he has killed the mourning dove.

21. They think that Byron should be proud of his natural African American hair and not try to change it.

22. His decision means that much of her careful planning for the journey was wasted. Furthermore, Momma fears that he has put them in danger by stopping at night in the mountains.

23. He goes there to see what Kenny is up to and to look after him.

24. Answers will vary. Perhaps it was someone who looked like Kenny, an angel, or an embodiment of Kenny's love for his sister. Later, believing Byron's opinion that some part of Kenny led Joey away from danger helps Kenny set aside the fear and guilt that have sent him into hiding.

25. The Epilogue gives more facts about the bombing. It also points out that the civil rights movement went on from that tragedy to help improve the lives of African Americans.

Part III: Essay Questions

Students should respond to two of the five essay questions. Answers will vary but should include specific references to the text.

a. The novel takes place in 1963 in Flint, Michigan, and Birmingham, Alabama. Students should recognize that the setting is crucial to the novel because some aspects of it, including the danger to African Americans traveling in the South and the civil unrest in Birmingham, drive the plot and influence the decisions made by the novel's characters.

b. Some students will say that the novel ends in sadness and fear, for a church has been bombed, four children have been killed, and Kenny has been depressed and living behind the family couch. Other students will say that it ends seriously but optimistically because Kenny comes out of his depression, recognizing that life goes on despite the ugliness. They might add that the Epilogue gives a final positive spin to the novel.

c. One explanation is that Byron finally has realized what his parents have been telling him—that life is serious and that he cannot make it if he doesn't change his behavior. Kenny, on the other hand, is just growing into the rebellious stage that Byron seems to be exiting. Kenny now wants to have adventures and test himself and the world.

d. Main themes for the novel include the power of prejudice and the importance of family. Students may suggest other themes, such as the difficulties of growing up or coming to terms with the evil in the world. They should provide details from different parts of the novel to support their view.

e. Answers will vary, but students may feel that the novel shed light on a historical period that they knew only from classroom study; that it helped them see how similar people are, despite differences of generation, location, or race; and that it reminded them that the support of one's family can help a person deal with the challenges in his or her life.